A Spiritual Growth Plan for Your Choleric Child

Connie Rossini

Four Waters Press
NEW ULM, MINNESOTA

Cover photo by fortherock, Flikr Creative Commons
www.flickr.com/photos/fortherock/3898642212/in/set-72157622170309749

© 2015 Four Waters Press
217 South Jefferson Street
New Ulm, Minnesota 56073

Ordering Information:
Special discounts are available on large-quantity purchases by parishes, book clubs, associations, and others. For details, contact the publisher at the address above.

Printed in the United States of America
First Printing, 2015

ISBN-13: 978-0692431566

To Dante,

my indefatigable choleric child,
with love and admiration for your determination to grow
closer to Christ.

Contents

Introduction

A Spiritual Growth Plan for Your Choleric Child had its beginning with the conception of the first of our four sons. He was full of energy even in the womb. I felt him moving by seventeen weeks gestation. Sometimes it seemed like he was turning somersaults. Once born, he rarely napped. He always wanted to be active. Before he could roll over or crawl, he liked to be carried around our apartment for hours. He had no stranger or separation anxiety. He began speaking at seven months. Long before that, he had an open-mouthed smile that reached ear to ear. He was determined to impact not only my husband and me, but the world.

I had our second son when the first was twenty months old. When I nursed the baby, our eldest would run by and hit him on the head. He spent much of his day throwing his toys down the stairs. I think he liked both the noise and the action.

It didn't take me long to see how different he was from me. But it did take me time to appreciate that difference. As a low-energy introvert, I was overwhelmed by his intensity, energy, and (when he got a little older) love of debating. I scoured parenting books for help. Eventually, I hit on the key: he was a choleric, as pure a choleric as I have yet come across. And I was a phlegmatic-melancholic.

Recently I began using knowledge of my children's temperaments to help them grow in their relationships with each other and with God. I have taken the initiative in our home, since I am primarily responsible for homeschooling our children. My husband helps refine my understanding of the temperaments, based on training he has received at work. He supports and encourages us, without being so involved in the daily details. Once a week we have temperament studies as part of our school day. I work one on one with each child, while another takes his piano lesson. During this time, we discuss any problems the child has had with his temperament over the last week. For the choleric child, I might ask, "How are you doing as a servant leader?" Or I might bring up concerns I have with his interaction with siblings. We read short stories or portions of longer books that showcase a character's good use or misuse of his temperament.

Since beginning this venture, our relationships with each of our children, and their relationships with each other, have deepened. We are each more apt to take the other's temperament into consideration when we disagree. We are changing our expectations and our perceptions of each other. It is a long-term project, but we are all growing close to Christ and to one another.

I would now like to share some of our successes with you, so that you can use them with your children.

This book is the first full-length volume in a series of four. I hope to follow it up with a book on each of the other three temperaments. While other books go into great detail about the distinctions between the temperaments, this series is a little different. After I publish the final volume, I plan to make a combined version that includes more background information, a temperament test (which you can also download free now through one of the links on my blog), and additional parenting tips for kids of each temperament.

However, my primary focus is to help you raise virtuous sons and daughters. I concentrate on children in elementary through junior high school, although you can adapt some of the suggestions to children who are older or younger.

Temperaments and Spiritual Growth

God made human beings in his image, with an intellect and a will. He made us to know and love him. He calls us to serve him with both our head and our heart. Knowledge of our temperaments helps us in several ways. It shows us that our problems are not unique. We can learn from others' successes and failures. Once we know the primary strengths and weaknesses of our temperament, we can use this knowledge to grow in virtue. We can focus our energy on combating the main fault of our temperament first, leaving lesser problems for a later time. Fr. Conrad Hock writes:

> One of the most reliable means of learning to know oneself is the study of the temperaments. For if a man is fully cognizant of his temperament, he can learn easily to direct and control himself. If he is able to discern the temperament of others, he can better understand and help them.[1]

Knowing our children's temperaments is similarly helpful. Sometimes we struggle to understand our children who have temperaments opposite to our own. When we learn about their temperaments, we not only learn to see things from their perspective, we also learn about their God-given strengths. We stop trying to remake them in our image and accept the image of God that they express through their temperament. On the other hand, recognizing

---

[1] Fr. Conrad Hock, *The Four Temperaments and the Spiritual Life,* (Milwaukee: Pallotine Brothers, 1934), *www.catholicapologetics.info/catholic-teaching/virtue/temperaments.htm*, 1:1 (accessed April 12, 2015).

that a child has a similar temperament to our own can help us watch out for problems we have struggled with. We can share what has worked for us, and what we are still trying to overcome. Whether our children are like us or completely different, we can encourage their special gifts and share stories of saints who were like themselves. We thus help them become more mature Christians and more effective servants of God.

Can We Really Help our Kids Grow Spiritually?

Another Catholic writer that I consulted while I was drafting this book contended that it was dangerous to expect much spiritual growth out of our children. We can't expect kids to be—well, adults. If we push them too far, they might run away from the faith.

Let's think about that for a minute. Consider academic subjects. If we push kids too far in math, some of them might grow to hate it. But we still require nearly all kids to learn the basics. Then when they get to senior high or beyond, they make the choice whether to continue studying math or not.

Spiritual growth is infinitely more important than mathematical knowledge. No, we shouldn't expect our first-graders to understand deep theology or be at an advanced stage of prayer. We should, however, help our children to grow up, both as humans and as Christians.

Pope St. John Paul II wrote about spiritual growth and the family:

> What is needed is a continuous, permanent conversion which, while requiring an interior detachment from every evil and an adherence to good in its fullness, is brought about concretely in steps which lead us ever forward. Thus a dynamic process develops, one which advances gradually with the progressive integra-

tion of the gifts of God and the demands of His definitive and absolute love in the entire personal and social life of man. Therefore an educational growth process is necessary, in order that individual believers, families and peoples, even civilization itself, by beginning from what they have already received of the mystery of Christ, may patiently be led forward, arriving at a richer understanding and a fuller integration of this mystery in their lives.[2]

This series is written to help families in that educational growth process, that patient leading forward of each member. Of course, we mold the religious formation to the child, his age, intellectual ability—and temperament. By focusing on temperament, I believe we do the best we can to make sure we don't push him farther than he can go. We make the faith attractive to him. We show him that we (and God) appreciate him for who he is. We give him the knowledge and the tools, and help him form the habits, that he needs to continue maturing in adulthood. We cannot make him a saint, but we can show him how to begin becoming one.

How to Use this Book

This book can be used by parents who are already well versed in the four temperaments and those who are just learning. Some of you will appreciate philosophical grounding. I begin with an overview of the four classic temperaments in chapter 1. Chapter 2 focuses on children who have a mixed choleric-sanguine or choleric-melancholic temperament. Chapter 3 discusses the meaning and means of spiritual growth. In chapters 4 through 11 you'll find specific suggestions to help your child grow in prayer and virtue, along with general teaching tips for homeschoolers in chapter 9. Chapter

---

[2] John Paul II, *Familiaris consortio*, Apostolic Exhortation on the Role of the Christian Family in the Modern World, Vatican Web site, *w2.vatican.va/content/john-paul-ii/en/apost_exhortations/documents/hf_jp-ii_exh_19811122_familiaris-consortio.html*, (accessed April 13, 2015), no. 8.

12 contains book lists and examples of saints and heroes who were cholerics. It also includes Bible verses for your child to memorize and longer portions of Scripture for him to study. Chapter 13 has detailed lesson plans for those who are in charge of their children's general or religious education. Chapter 14 contains the templates and printouts you need to plan your temperament studies. Feel free to use whichever parts of the book fit your needs.

For ease of reading, I use the traditional pronouns "he" and "him," et cetera, throughout the book. I am sure the reader will understand that I am writing for parents of both boys and girls. Likewise, I assume that most of my readers are part of a married couple and the text reflects that. I mean no slight to single parents, who should be able to adapt my recommendations to their situations.

CHAPTER 1

The Choleric Temperament

The Greek physician Hippocrates (from whom we get the Hippocratic Oath) first proposed the four temperaments in the fourth century B.C. He believed that bodily fluids help determine how individuals react to stimuli. Finding four basic patterns of reactions, he related them to four bodily fluids or humors, calling them choleric, sanguine, phlegmatic, and melancholic. A later physician named Galen refined this theory. Today we no longer view the temperaments as rooted in bodily fluids. However, many psychologists and Catholic theologians continue to promote the four temperament divisions Hippocrates observed.

As Hippocrates noted, some people respond to stimuli without thinking. Others need time to reflect. Some people's reaction to stimuli endures. Others' reaction soon fades. Experts often call these differences "degrees of excitability." Cholerics have quick and lasting reactions. Sanguines react quickly, but their feelings fade almost at once. These are the two extroverted temperaments. Phlegmatics react slowly with fading feelings. Melancholics also react slowly, but their reactions last. Phlegmatics and melancholics are introverts.

I like to think of the temperaments as four squares within a larger square. Starting with the top left and proceeding clockwise, the four temperaments are choleric, sanguine, phlegmatic, and melancholic. The two top squares are the extroverted temperaments. The two bottom squares are the introverted. The two right squares have short-lived reactions. The two left squares have long-lived.

Choleric quick reaction long-lived impression	Sanguine quick reaction short-lived impression
Melancholic slow reaction long-lived impression	Phlegmatic slow reaction short-lived impression

Does Everyone Have One of these Temperaments?

Besides the four pure temperaments, there are also mixed temperaments. Many people are choleric-sanguine, sanguine-phlegmatic, phlegmatic-melancholic, or melancholic-choleric. Some people appear to have a few characteristics of a third temperament. Experts disagree on whether a third temperament is possible. What appears to be a third temperament could actually be habits of behavior influenced by one's environment. Most authorities agree that a healthy person would not be evenly split between two opposite temperaments. A sanguine-melancholic, for instance, would probably be an unhealthy personality.

Temperaments are genetic, but that does not mean that all members of a family will have the same temperament, just as they will not necessarily all have the same hair color. For example, my father is sanguine-choleric and my mother is choleric-melancholic. Yet I and most of my siblings are phlegmatic, melancholic, or a combination of the two. Only two out of nine of us are strongly choleric. On the other hand, I know of some families in which almost everyone has the same temperament.

What about Other Temperament Systems?

Googling "temperaments" results in a host of websites with different temperament systems. Many of these systems are broadly based on behavior, not specifically on reaction to stimuli. They thus draw the lines between temperaments differently than Hippocrates did. Some of them appear to be descriptions of personalities, rather than temperaments. What is the difference? Fr. Jordan Aumann, OP, writes:

> We must ... consider the human person in terms of temperaments and character, which are the basic elements that constitute personhood... Heredity is the fundamental source of temperament, and environment is the basic causal factor of character.[3]

---

[3] Jordan Aumann, OP, *Spiritual Theology, achive.org/stream/SpiritualTheology-ByFr.JordanAumannO.p/AumannO.p.SpiritualTheologyall_djvu.tx*t, (accessed April 12, 2015), 2:7.

Personality is comprised of temperament and character. Temperament is inborn and unchangeable. Although a person can certainly learn to control his temperament (or I would not have written this book), he can never acquire a different temperament. Personality, on the other hand, includes many factors, temperament being just one. Personality is formed by a combination of heredity, family structure, culture, health, religion, education, and habits. It develops over a lifetime as we respond to forces outside ourselves.

Here are a few alternate temperament or personality systems you may encounter:

- The DISC system modernizes Hippocrates' four classic temperaments, using descriptions we can more easily understand. Some businesses use this system to help employees and their bosses understand each other better. D stands for Dominant and is another name for choleric. I stands for Influential and is another name for sanguine. S stands for Steady and is another name for phlegmatic. C stands for Conscientious and is another name for melancholic. The Catholic Leadership Institute has adapted the DISC system specifically for Catholic organizations and dioceses.

- In the 1980s a group of Christian counselors suggested a fifth temperament, called supine. They also redefined the meaning of the phlegmatic temperament. Most Catholic authorities would say people who self-identify as supine are one of the four classic temperaments (and perhaps a lesser mix of others), but either misunderstand themselves or the makeup of the temperaments. Another possibility is that these individuals suffer from some form of mental illness.

- The Myers-Briggs Type Indicator (MBTI) is a popular personality test based on Jungian psychology.

- The Keirsey Temperament Sorter is psychologist David Keirsey's attempt to reconcile the MBTI with the four classic temperaments. Keirsey calls the four temperaments Artisan, Guardian, Rational, and Idealist. He breaks each of these down into four sub-types. However, it is difficult to match these types with the distinctions of the four classic temperaments. I have seen different authors correlate the same of Keirsey's types with different temperaments. The types are based on a person's motivations, not his reaction to stimuli. While each temperament needs to be motivated in a different manner, interior motivations are not at the root of temperamental differences. Keirsey includes both introverts and extroverts in each of his types.

- Educators and pediatricians have their own temperament systems for children. These largely stem from the New York Longitudinal Study of the 1950s and beyond, headed by Alexander Thomas and Stella Chess. Thomas and Chess observed nine traits in children: activity level, rhythmicity, adaptability, sensitivity, reaction to new people or situations, intensity, mood, distractibility, and attention span. They then grouped children into three types based on these traits: difficult, easy, and slow to warm up. Even from the names given to these types it appears that adults' perceptions of children were a key factor in the divisions.

How is Temperament Related to Behavior?

How do we know that the classic temperament system is more accurate than personality-based models? Can we really correlate a whole swath of behaviors with a specific type of reaction to stimuli?

We are not discussing dogma when we discuss the temperaments. There is room for disagreement. However, I have found the classic temperament divisions to work for virtually everyone who understands them and understands themselves. Here is how certain behaviors are connected to a specific temperament.

The choleric reacts quickly with strong and lasting impressions. Since his impressions last, he is determined to stick to his original way of seeing things. He does not change his perspective easily. He has a hard time letting go of arguments. His anger can be explosive and lasts a long time. He responds negatively to ideas other than his own. If he can see a way of making an idea his own, adding his input or incorporating it into his personal goals, he can then embrace it. He learns what he really thinks by talking about it. Arguing refines his thought. Since he is outwardly focused and persistent, he has great physical energy.

The sanguine reacts strongly and at once, but is moved just as strongly by the next stimuli, and so puts the past reaction aside. He is highly distractible. He wants to move on after a disagreement, and help others to do the same, so he'll urge them to overcome their differences. Since he runs from one impression to the next, he lacks commitment. He makes friends easily, but few of his friendships are deep. He does not think ahead and has a hard time learning from his mistakes. He eagerly embraces a new project, but rarely follows through to the end.

The phlegmatic reacts slowly and mildly and does not hang onto impressions. He is inwardly focused and peaceful within himself. Conflict upsets him. It moves him against his will. He acts based on how his actions will affect his and others' peace. Physical activity wears him out quickly, as does too much talking. He may even find intellectual work too taxing. He has difficulty making decisions. He is out of touch with his feelings and has trouble expressing them.

The melancholic reacts slowly, but retains his impressions. He may overlook a first offense or even a second. But by the third, his anger often boils over. He has a long memory and difficulty forgiving wrongs. He perseveres in his commitments. He takes rules seriously. He has few friendships, but they are deep. He is thoughtful and serious. He will stick with a job until it is finished, feeling that the burden to complete it is on him. He can be too hard on himself and others.

Each of the characteristics we associate with a particular temperament is a manifestation of reaction to stimuli. These reactions are inborn. However, we can learn to regulate our behavior so that we can minimize the negative behaviors associated with our temperament. We can also learn how to use our temperament for positive good.

What Distinguishes the Choleric Temperament?

The choleric temperament is usually the easiest of the four to identify. As the parent of a choleric child, you have likely noticed his intensity all his life. The choleric infant often cries or screams at birth. He may be colicky. He bursts with energy. He keeps his parents up at night and does not like to nap. He demands full-time attention.

He is a natural leader. He has grandiose dreams. He loves to be in charge. Give him a task that interests him, and he will eagerly pursue it on his own. He likes to rally others to his cause and direct them towards a common goal. Although he is an extrovert, he does not just "hang out" with friends, chit-chatting. In social situations, he often has an agenda. It can be as simple as persuading others to play a board game that he really wants to play. He is decisive, outgoing, and self-confident. He is seldom afraid to stand up for the truth. He rarely gives in to peer pressure. He tends to speak and act without thinking.

In his relationships, the choleric is generous with his possessions and likes to help others with physical tasks. At the same time, he may be insensitive to others' feelings. Although generally optimistic about life and his prospects for success, he gets angry easily and can be physically violent. He often cuts down his opponents with harsh words. He has a difficult time admitting he is wrong. He might lie, exaggerate, or hide or twist the truth to appear innocent. He also dislikes discussing his emotions. He does not brood, but his negative impressions of other people or things last a long time. He may seek revenge on those who have hurt him. He desires to see people who break the rules brought to justice.

The hardest thing for him may be to sit and do nothing—and say nothing. He must always be active, especially doing something with his hands. If he is not talking, he likes to be writing his thoughts or plans. He enjoys having others in the room with him while he does it, provided they don't try to distract him from his agenda. If he gets a new idea, he wants to implement it at once. He sees the big picture and likes to recruit others to help him with the details.

The choleric child is sometimes called spirited, strong-willed, or high strung. He tends to move quickly. His eyes reveal his determination, energy, and self-confidence. He is typically good at sports. As a pure extrovert he is energized by being with people. If he spends too much time alone, too much time being quiet, he might start acting out. He will be more easily angered, more apt to argue or disobey, more likely to yell or lash out. It's important to recall that every choleric child is different. Some may have all the characteristics I've listed, others may have most. What sets the choleric apart is his reaction to stimuli. Remember, the choleric responds immediately to stimuli that come to him through his senses. He reacts strongly, and has a hard time putting his reactions aside. If something reminds him of an incident, his reaction could repeat itself.

Destined to Make a Difference

Your choleric child has a shrewd mind. He takes in many sensory cues around him without even thinking about them, so that he seems to have special intuition at times. Every time I watch a mystery show with my choleric mother, she guesses who the perpetrator is within the first half hour—before we see most of the clues. She is always right. My choleric son appears to have the same talent.

This keen awareness helps your child get himself out of many scrapes. He can make decisions without having to think first and they are often the same decisions a more reflective person would have come to over time. This ability to think on his feet will help him be the first to take advantage of new opportunities. He could easily become one of the early investors in a company that later is hugely successful. He might be the first to try new technology, the first to exploit new discoveries. He will also be good at avoiding traffic tickets and accidents, even though his driving might terrify you.[4]

---

[4] Tim LaHaye, *Spirit-Controlled Temperament,* (La Mesa, CA: Post, 1993), 20.

The choleric is the most likely temperament to make a noticeable difference in the world. He may be famous or infamous. Fr. Conrad Hock and Fr. Jordan Aumann have both said that the choleric (perhaps together with the melancholic) is the most likely to become a saint.[5] He is also the most likely to become a tyrant.

God placed an awesome responsibility in your hands when he gave you this child. It is your job to help him overcome the tendencies that could make him a tyrant and strengthen the tendencies that could make him a saint. But don't worry! God never gives a responsibility without giving the grace and aid to complete it. Even when you make mistakes, God will be there to make good come out of them.

---

[5] Aumann, *2:7*. Also Hock, 1:3.

CHAPTER 2

Children with Mixed Temperaments

S ome people are completely choleric by temperament, or have only one or two characteristics of another temperament. They are easiest to identify and understand. Many more people have a mixed temperament, with choleric being part of it. Due to the mix, it is more difficult to pinpoint their temperament or to predict how they might act in a particular circumstance. An almost infinite number of subtle differences exist between people.

In this chapter, I will discuss choleric-sanguine and choleric-melancholic mixes as they relate to parenting, teaching, and especially the spiritual life. If you have a child with a mixed temperament, keep these suggestions in mind as you read the rest of this book. I will be focusing on the pure choleric temperament for the remainder of the book, since I could never enumerate all the possible variations.

People with mixed temperaments are often happier and more balanced than those with a pure temperament. They are more sympathetic to others' viewpoints, since they themselves do not always see things from one narrow perspective. Author Florence Littauer contends that people who have two horizontally connected temperaments on the temperament square are more balanced than those whose temperaments connect vertically.[6] In other words, a choleric-sanguine, who has two extroverted temperaments, will be more balanced than a choleric-melancholic, who shares characteristics of both extroversion and introversion. Why would this be so? Both the choleric and melancholic focus on ideas and logic and hang onto their impressions for a long time. The sanguine, on the other hand, is a people person who easily shrugs off past hurts.

What about opposite temperaments? Many writers about the four temperaments, including Fr. Conrad Hock and Protestant author Tim LaHaye, believe that some people have a choleric-phlegmatic temperament. Art and Laraine Bennett argue that this is not possible and I agree with them.[7] If we recall that temperaments are based on reaction to stimuli, the near-impossibility of opposite combinations becomes clear. It's not just a matter of someone sometimes getting violently angry and at other times showing no emotion at all. Rather, a choleric-phlegmatic combination would mean innately reacting quickly and vehemently to stimuli and hanging onto that reaction in some situations, and reacting slowly and mildly and quickly forgetting in other situations. Such varied reactions would not usually (if ever) exist in a healthy person.

Why then can a person seem to be both choleric and phlegmatic? First and most obviously, a person who thinks he is choleric-phlegmatic may not understand himself. Perhaps he is looking at his

---

[6] Florence Littauer, *Personality Plus for Couples: Understanding Yourself and the One You Love,* (Grand Rapids, MI: F.H. Revell, 2001), 64.
[7] Art and Laraine Bennett, *The Temperament God Gave You: The Classic Key to Knowing Yourself, Getting along with Others, and Growing Closer to the Lord,* (Manchester, NH: Sophia Institute Press, 2005), 199-200.

behavior only, and not getting to the roots of why he is reacting in a certain way.

He may misunderstand where to draw the dividing line between various temperaments. Sometimes people will modify their natural tendencies because they are working on personal or spiritual growth. Or a child might learn to imitate the habits of his parents who have a different temperament than his. He may mask his true temperament to please others or to make his life easier. A choleric daughter of two choleric parents, for example, may not feel free to be herself. Her parents give her few opportunities to be in control. They stamp out her protests and arguments. She begins suppressing her natural tendencies to react quickly and strongly, and appears to be phlegmatic. She is not at peace doing so. When she is away from her parents, her real temperament manifests itself. She and others become confused about what her temperament is.

Another problem arises from temperament tests. Many tests that rely on adjectives fail to define them. A reader's understanding of "stubborn," for example, may not be the same as the test maker's. Other temperament tests rely on questions about how a person acts in specific situations. These actions may be influenced by not only temperament, but family upbringing, habit, culture, and peer pressure. In other words, a choleric may not act like a choleric in all situations, especially in those where he does not feel free to be himself.

All of this can make it hard to pinpoint not only an adult's primary temperament, but also his secondary temperament, if any. On the other hand, as a parent working with your young child, you probably know his temperament quite well. You can recall what he was like in his first moments, and you have witnessed distinct patterns of behavior.

Most cholerics will have a secondary temperament that is either sanguine or melancholic, although my experience is that about 10 to 20 percent of people have a pure or nearly pure temperament. Here are some tips for working with your child who has a blended temperament. Remember, each child will have a slightly different blend, creating great variety. I will generalize for simplicity.

Choleric-Sanguines

Cholerics and sanguines are both extroverts. They both discover what they think by talking. They both like to spend most of their time with other people and are energized by doing so. Neither is very reflective. Combinations between the two are very outgoing. Most authors agree that the sanguine-choleric temperament is the most talkative, the typical salesman. Sanguine-cholerics react quickly and sometimes harshly, but they just as quickly repent of any rash words.

The choleric-sanguine is somewhat different. He not only reacts quickly and strongly, in most cases he holds onto his feelings for a long time.

But this combination will be more cheerful and more people-oriented than a pure choleric. He uses his personal charm to persuade others to join his cause. On the other hand, he is even less likely than the pure choleric to think before he speaks. He tends to cut down his opponent or build himself up without thinking about the long-term consequences. He uses his peacemaking skills to persuade others he is truly sorry so that they give him another chance. Over time, he may bruise others once too often, so that they refuse to be on his team any longer. This pattern could repeat itself until he finally loses friends or colleagues for good.

Personal coach and teacher Hal Warfield describes this temperament mix very well:

> The second strongest extrovert is an active and purposeful individual. He is almost fearless and has high levels of energy. Whatever his profession, his brain is always active and engaged. His weaknesses combine the quick anger of the sanguine with the resentment of the choleric. He gets AND gives ulcers. He may leave people, including spouse and children, shell-shocked and resentful of his angry outbursts.[8]

Another major issue for the choleric-sanguine is superficiality. Combine the choleric's lack of connection with his feelings with the sanguine's tendency to bounce from one stimulus to the next, and you'll likely have someone with a shallow interior life. This can be devastating to his spiritual growth. Even more so than the pure choleric, he needs spiritual direction.

As a parent, model early and often the joy of reading. Supply your child with lots of exciting stories filled with interesting characters. Read aloud to him all through his school years, even reading aloud once a week as a family when he is in high school. Sunday evenings are the perfect time for this, around a fireplace if possible. Read books together that challenge your choleric-sanguine to reflect on important issues, especially moral issues.

Stories about how real people overcame temptation and stood strong for the truth can inspire your choleric-sanguine to stand fast against the world. He may be drawn to designing projects that will help others. Encourage his leadership qualities. Help him practice the corporal works of mercy, which I talk about in chapter 3 and Lesson Plan 5.

---

[8] Hal Warfield, "Temperament and Personality," *Selfgrowth*, *www.selfgrowth.com/articles/Warfield2.html*, (accessed April 12, 2015).

More than the pure choleric, the child with this blend may need guidance in choosing the right short-term and long-term goals. Help him form an image of the person he would like to be. How can he reach his goal?

The choleric-sanguine will express sadness and other emotions more easily than the pure choleric. You may have to teach him to be more guarded in sharing what he feels. He will not have many inhibitions towards strangers. His desire for adventure and lack of reflection could make him a daredevil. He might be fearless to a fault.

A father can help his choleric-sanguine daughter to see the importance of modesty and guarding her heart. He can teach her survival skills and self-defense. The two could even take a martial arts class together, the father making sure that they chose an instructor who steers clear of eastern spirituality and sticks to the art.

A choleric father will often clash with his choleric-sanguine child, but this child needs lots of affection. Do not be afraid to be demonstrative, even with your choleric-sanguine son. Your child will love compliments, either on his skills, his character, or his appearance, depending on the individual. Ample praise and frequent hugs will promote good will between you.

The choleric-sanguine child grows bored easily. In school, he needs to have short and interesting classes with lots of hands-on activities and movement if possible. Physical education may be his favorite class. He will need lots of time with friends. Get him involved in sports, dance class, gymnastics, or clubs.

He may dislike spending time cleaning and organizing. You may have to motivate him to keep his room clean with socializing opportunities or reward systems. The sanguine side of his temperament will want to please you and imitate you, so the more diligent you are in household chores, the more likely he will follow suit.

St. Thomas Beckett was probably a choleric-sanguine. As a young man he loved fine and beautiful things, but he became ascetical after he was ordained archbishop of Canterbury. His anger and pride were not so easy to overcome. He clashed with King Henry II and would not compromise. This clash eventually ended in Thomas's martyrdom.

The choleric-sanguine should memorize and put into practice the teaching of Romans 12:

> Do not be conformed to this world but be transformed by the renewal of your mind, that you may prove what is the will of God, what is good and acceptable and perfect... Let love be genuine; hate what is evil, hold fast to what is good... be patient in tribulation, be constant in prayer. Contribute to the needs of the saints, practice hospitality... Do not be overcome by evil, but overcome evil with good.[9]

Choleric-Melancholics

The choleric-melancholic may be the most successful leader. He knows what his goals are, he is determined to reach them, and he pays close attention to the details that a pure choleric would overlook or leave to others. He is a hardworking, driven perfectionist. He is less talkative and more reflective than a pure choleric. He might even be shy in large groups, while still needing to speak in order to know his own mind and preferring being with others to spending time alone.

The choleric-melancholic child can be very organized with a perfectly ordered room and closet. He loves making lists and charts and using calendars and planners. But he wants things organized his way. Don't try to tell him which drawer to put his shirts in!

---

[9] Rom 12: 2, 9, 12, 13, and 21.

A choleric-melancholic daughter can be a great help to her mother. From an early age she may want to earn extra money to save up for special purchases by babysitting younger siblings. She can generally be relied on to do a good job. If she babysits for neighbors, they may come home to find she has done the dishes as well. She may love being in charge of planning and making meals for the family. But she will have no patience with siblings who don't like what she fixes.

If your oldest child is choleric-melancholic, he will set the tone for the rest of the family. You may have the neatest home of all your friends.

The choleric-melancholic can also be very negative. He tends to focus on what is wrong with a situation, rather than what is right. When others show no interest in helping him achieve his goals, he may begin to despair. He has a strong desire to control not only his environment, but also the people in it. He may even complain that he cannot control people!

He also tends to be self-absorbed. He almost always thinks or talks about himself or his plans. He may be a chronic interrupter and poor listener. He is easily offended and forgives with difficulty. He is judgmental and may constantly talk about what others are doing wrong or what's wrong with the world.

As the parent of a choleric-melancholic, challenge your child to do something to right the wrongs he sees, rather than just complaining about them. Ask for his opinion and help in making your household run more smoothly.

If you are a phlegmatic parent, you may be tempted to let him criticize your lack of organization and drive. Preempt him by telling him how much you appreciate his skills and by putting him in charge of chores you dislike or are not good at. If you have a choleric or melancholic temperament, or a blend of the two, your child can be a great partner to you if you can agree on goals that are important to both of you.

Every temperament may use manipulation, but the choleric-melancholic can be a master of it. He may use both explosive anger and moodiness to get his way.[10] He is the king of the guilt-trip, especially toward other melancholics. He uses their sense of duty to make them feel like they have no choice but to do what he asks. He may try to run every aspect of his siblings' lives.

St. Paul was probably a choleric-melancholic. He was determined, principled, and hard working. He stood fast for the truth and persuaded thousands to follow Christ. At the same time, he had to learn a life-changing lesson in humility. He was convinced he was right to the point of overseeing the death of St. Stephen. He relentlessly pursued the early Christians, until God intervened. When he realized how wrong he had been, he was tempted to despair. The choleric-melancholic should make these words of St. Paul his motto: "I can do all things through Christ who strengthens me" (Phil 4:13). His greatest danger is self-absorption. He can either think he knows everything (pride) or be in despair that he doesn't.

He needs to learn to place his trust solely in the goodness of God. St. Therese's little way of spiritual childhood may seem too emotion-based to him, although Therese herself was probably melancholic. But St. Paul can be his hero. The entire book of Philippians can teach him to be humble and joyful. You might start by having him memorize this passage:

> Do nothing from selfishness or conceit, but in humility count others better than yourselves. Let each of you look not only to his own interests, but also to the interests of others. Have this mind among yourselves, which is yours in Christ Jesus, who, though he was in the form of God, did not count equality with God a thing to be grasped, but emptied himself, taking the form of a servant,

---

[10] See Littauer, 22.

being born in the likeness of men. And being found in human form he humbled himself and became obedient unto death, even death on a cross. Therefore God has highly exalted him and bestowed on him the name which is above every name, that at the name of Jesus every knee should bow, in heaven and on earth and under the earth, and every tongue confess that Jesus Christ is Lord, to the glory of God the Father.[11]

Choleric-melancholic girls may find a heroine in St. Joan of Arc, who fearlessly led men into battle, but became filled with self-doubt when put on trial.

Among the spiritual works of mercy, instructing the ignorant and admonishing sinners will probably come naturally to the choleric-melancholic. Encourage him also to practice bearing wrongs patiently and forgiving offenses willingly. Books and movies that show the motivations of people who make mistakes can teach him sympathy for those who sin against him. A daily examination of conscience is indispensable.

The choleric-melancholic will hate it when people tell him to "lighten up," but you should encourage him to try some less-serious activities. His melancholic side is poetic. Introduce him to great art, music, and theater. Encourage him to share his ideals with the world through writing. A sanguine parent can teach him the virtues of small talk—but be careful here. Too much idle chatter will turn him off to the idea. Show him how interest in other's lives can help him further his goals.

---

[11] Phil 2:3-11.

CHAPTER 3

The Meaning and Means of Spiritual Growth

W hat is "spiritual growth?" How can people grow spiritually? What is the goal of the spiritual life? Before trying to help your child grow spiritually, you should know the answers to these questions.

The Fathers of the Second Vatican Council wrote:

> All Christians in any state or walk of life are called to the fullness of Christian life and to the perfection of charity.[12]

Notice it says "all Christians," and "the fullness of Christian life." Your child is not called to be a mediocre Christian. He is not called to climb half way up the mountain to God. He is called to "the *perfection* of Christian charity." In other words, God wants your child to become a saint. Your child is called to love God with his whole heart, mind, soul, and strength and his neighbor as himself.[13]

Your child has his own will. As a choleric, he has a very strong will. You cannot force him to do anything. You can make many spir-

---

[12] *Lumen Gentium* no. 40 § 2, quoted in CCC 2013.
[13] See Mt 22:37-40.

itual growth plans for him, but you cannot change his heart. He must choose to work with God's grace to become holy. But if you follow the suggestions in this book, you will increase the likelihood that he will choose holiness. In forming your child's mind and heart, you must respect his God-given freedom. Working with his temperament should help you in the endeavor.

Formation of Conscience

Conversion is a life-long process. There is always room for more knowledge, more conforming of the will to God. There is always room for love to be more perfect. You are helping your child start on the road to God. He must see it through to the end.

As you teach your child right from wrong, how to love God and others, you help him to form his conscience. A well-formed conscience enables him to choose good and reject evil. It helps him overcome temptation throughout his life.

Besides the intellectual formation of knowing what is right, your child needs to form habits of virtuous behavior. The habits of childhood can last a lifetime. When these habits are reinforced by the virtuous examples of others, they provide the foundation for a rich spiritual life.

The Catechism of the Catholic Church says:

> It is important for every person to be sufficiently present to himself in order to hear and follow the voice of his conscience, This requirement of *interiority* is all the more necessary as life often distracts us from any reflection, self-examination, or introspection.[14]

14 CCC 1779.

Studying and working on temperamental issues with your child can lead him to be more reflective, so that he can hear the voice of his conscience and respond to it. The Catechism continues:

> The education of the conscience is a lifelong task. From the earliest years, it awakens the child to the knowledge and practice of the interior law recognized by conscience. Prudent education teaches virtue; it prevents or cures fear, selfishness and pride, resentment arising from guilt, and feelings of complacency, born of human weakness and faults. The education of the conscience guarantees freedom and engenders peace of heart.[15]

Isn't that what we all want for our children?

Growing in Intimacy with Christ

Christian perfection is not just a matter of moral righteousness. It is a matter of love. The goal of the spiritual life is an intimate relationship with God through Jesus Christ. Your child will grow in virtue not just through his human effort, but by cooperating with God's grace. Grace comes to us when we obey God's will, when we spend time in prayer, and especially through the sacraments.

> A virtue is an [sic] habitual and firm disposition to do the good. It allows the person not only to perform good acts, but to give the best of himself. The virtuous person tends toward the good with all his sensory and spiritual powers; he pursues the good and chooses it in concrete actions.[16]

You can measure your child's spiritual growth, to a certain extent, by his effort to overcome his faults, his desire to pray and the care he takes in praying, and his love for the Mass and the Sacrament of Reconciliation. At the same time, spiritual growth, since it is

---

[15] CCC 1784.
[16] CCC 1803.

growth in intimacy with Christ, is a secret, mysterious process. Only God can discern how much your child is taking the faith to heart, rather than just conforming outwardly to the behavior he believes you want to see.

Your child's psychological maturity will have a great impact on his relationship with God. The more he matures a as a person, the deeper his love relationship with Christ can become. We cannot expect him to love God at a level that is beyond the capacity of his years. Children are self-centered. God designs them this way to ensure that they receive the love and care they need for survival and lifelong happiness. As long as your child sees you and your spouse primarily through the lens of his needs, he will see God the same way. He will see God as someone who supplies for his needs and wants. This is normal and healthy.

In adolescence, he will begin to look at God more analytically. He will ask questions and desire answers. He will enjoy finding logical reasons for the faith. He will try to understand God's character at a deeper level.[17] As part of growing up, he will go through a period of questioning what you have taught him. Try to see this period as an opportunity for great spiritual growth in your child, rather than something for you to fear. Your prayers and sacrifices for your child, as well as your love, understanding, and example, can help him make the faith his own.

Steps in Spiritual Change

Before you can motivate your child to change, you should understand how people are motivated. Each temperament requires a slightly different motivation technique, yet everyone shares some

---

[17] Fr. Benedict Groeschel provides an excellent explanation of these stages in his book *Spiritual Passages: The Psychology of Spiritual Development.*

basic similarities. Over the years, I have come to recognize several steps that I go through before I make a major change in my spiritual life. I used to believe that cholerics were unteachable, largely because I was going about things the wrong way. My successes with my son have made me see that he too follows the same steps.

1. Someone else's idea

When helping your choleric child to change, you must first tell him what the goal is. Show him it is important by practicing it yourself. If you want to teach him to pray, pray. If you want to teach him empathy, show concern when he is disappointed. This instruction and modeling only comprises the first step towards his making a change.

2. Conviction that a change is necessary

The movement from a vague awareness that others think you should change, to conviction that you must, often results from a crisis. For example, a boy who never listened to his mother when she said he needed to learn to swim might be suddenly motivated after he nearly drowns. He realizes she was right!

Art and Laraine Bennett, authors of *The Temperament God Gave You,* describe this step as being able to change. They say a person must believe he can succeed before he will make a commitment.[18] When trying to form your child's character, give him lots of encouragement, share examples of others who have succeeded, and remind him of past successes.

For a choleric, self-confidence is not usually the problem it can be with other temperaments. He is more likely to think the steps too slow, wanting to mount them two at a time. What he really needs is

---

[18] Bennetts, 169.

to make the conviction his own. He needs it to be his personal goal, not just your goal for him.

The choleric values logic and reason. Show him facts. Give him Scripture verses to memorize that exemplify the goal. Better yet, assign him to research why he needs to be compassionate or patient or humble. Use the Bible and the Catechism as sources. Have him brainstorm reasons the virtue you want him to embrace is important. *Let him convince himself.*

3. The will to change

Once a person is convinced of the need for change, he must choose it. At first he chooses the overall goal of change. Then he must choose to follow through when temptations or distractions plague him.

Other people can help with the first two steps. With the third a person is on his own—except, of course, for grace. Only you can make the choice to change your life. Only your child can make the choice to change his. But you can help your child strengthen his will, making it more likely he will choose the change you are proposing.

Prayer is at the root of all true spiritual change, because prayer brings your child into God's presence. In prayer (whether the liturgy of the Church or personal prayer), he meets God. He learns about God's goodness. His heart is moved to follow God's will. God gives him the grace to say *yes*. This is particularly true of meditation on Sacred Scripture. It informs your child's mind, moves his will, and opens his heart to grace. Begin working with your child to learn how to practice mental prayer as early as possible. Later in this book I give you several helps to do this.

Also for this step, motivate your child with stories of admirable people who made the right choices. Use the lives of choleric saints and heroes as examples. These stories will touch his heart. An older child can write "what-if" stories: What if St. Paul had refused to preach to the Gentiles, feeling this was beneath his dignity as a Jew? What if Mother Angelica had not accepted her mother as a postulant in her new order of sisters? Alternatively, choose an infamous choleric who chose not to embrace virtue, and have your choleric rewrite the story. What if Queen Jezebel had repented when Elijah spoke against her? What if Cain had tried to be more like Abel, instead of being envious? You can use fables and morality tales such as those in *The Book of Virtues* or books from the book list for this purpose. You can adapt this exercise for elementary school children by discussing the stories orally.

A choleric sometimes needs to be shown how a change will benefit him. For example, if he learns to praise rather than criticize others, they will more willingly join in his cause. If he learns to argue fairly and calmly, you will listen to his point of view. If he becomes humble, he could be a great saint. If you are not choleric yourself, you may find it distasteful to have to address the "what's-in-it-for-me" question. Try not to see this as a selfish question, but just the way your child's mind works. It is useless to try to motivate him as if he were a sanguine, phlegmatic, or melancholic.

Another suggestion coming from Art and Laraine Bennett is issuing a challenge as a motivating factor.[19] I have seen this work in many areas with my choleric.

4. Specific goals

Once your child has decided to change, he needs to choose concrete goals to make that change. Help him start small. It is better for him to take baby steps and succeed than to try giant leaps and keep failing. Your choleric child will constantly try to run ahead of you (liter-

---

[19] Bennetts, 177.

ally and figuratively). Don't let him take off so quickly that he misses some important elements of prayer, for example. You don't want him to form bad habits that he will later have to break. Once he has formed some basic good habits, he can move on more quickly.

Be patient with your child. Real change does not happen overnight. The start of the road has the roughest terrain. "At the proper time, you will reap a harvest, if you do not give up."[20]

---

[20] Gal 6:9.

CHAPTER 4

Modeling God's Fatherhood

The family is a domestic church, the Church in miniature.

> The Christian home is the place where children receive the first proclamation of the faith. For this reason the family home is rightly called "the domestic church," a community of grace and prayer, a school of human virtues and of Christian charity. [21]

God designed the domestic church to begin forming children in love of God and neighbor. In your family, you and your spouse stand in the place of God for your children. You give them their first glimpse of God's fatherhood and his loving care for his children. You teach them the importance of obedience to authority, especially divine authority. Likewise, siblings teach each other how to love their neighbors as themselves. As a whole family, you instill the idea that the spiritual life is not meant to be lived in isolation. It is not just a matter of "me and God," but of being a member of God's family.

Over the next several chapters, we will explore the relationship between you and your choleric child, his relationship with his siblings, and his relationship with the larger world. We will also con-

---

[21] CCC 1666.

sider how you can lead him to greater self-control and how the atmosphere of your home should reflect an authentic Catholic culture.

Parental Temperaments

Every Christian can benefit from having a spiritual director, but the choleric should especially learn to bow to a director. A good director can help him overcome his pride, see all his strengths as God's gifts, and learn the compassion that will keep him from becoming a tyrant.[22] In his childhood years, you are his spiritual director.

If your direction is going to benefit your child, he must respect you and see you as his ally. It is easy for parents with a different temperament to be overly critical of the choleric. Sanguine, phlegmatic, and melancholic parents will each have different issues.

The sanguine parent resembles the choleric in speaking without thinking and loving to spend time with others. The sanguine, however, may not understand that his choleric child holds onto hurts. When someone criticizes the sanguine, he may lash out immediately, but then quickly put the incident behind him. The sanguine parent and choleric child can easily trade barbs. The parent shrugs off the exchange, but the child holds onto his anger and bruised ego. The sanguine parent must make sure to apologize so the child knows he harbors no ill feelings. Taming the tongue is something they can work on together. The sanguine parent should also avoid challenging his child for the limelight, especially in areas in which the child excels.

The phlegmatic parent will find himself exhausted and overwhelmed by his choleric child. He hates conflict and it appears to him that the choleric loves it. He loves quiet and his child is rarely quiet. He has low energy and his child never stops moving until he

---

[22] See Hock, 1:4.

drops. This parent needs to know when to put space between him and his child. He needs another adult—preferably his spouse—to back him up on rules and discipline. He must guard against using passive-aggressive anger to punish his child for misbehavior he neglected to correct. He and his child can work together on recognizing and expressing their emotions in a healthy manner.

The melancholic parent shares the choleric child's desire for greatness. They both focus on ideas or projects rather than people. The melancholic parent should be careful not to expect adult behavior from one so young. He should look to his own failings and shortcomings so that he is not too hard on the child. He should strive to compliment the good he sees, while still encouraging the child to reach his full potential. The melancholic parent needs plenty of rest in order to overcome his tendency to despair and to have a slow build of anger. He also needs time away from relating to his child. This parent-child combination can be wonderful at helping each other grow in holiness, but the melancholic needs to make sure his child is not always the leader.

The Importance of Fathers

One of the determining factors on whether a choleric becomes famous or infamous may be his relationship with his father. Hitler, Stalin, Idi Amin, and Mao Zedong, among others, all had absentee or abusive fathers.

In most families, the mother will be the one to spend time working with the kids on temperament issues. When this is the case, the father should find a separate special time to spend alone with each child. This gives both parents a concrete opportunity to help their children grow spiritually. Otherwise, doing so could remain a wish that never gets fulfilled or a vague goal that is never realized. Your child needs his father to take an active role in his spiritual development!

Once our boys hit age nine or ten, they take turns going for walks with my husband. They discuss anything that is on their mind, but especially private struggles, or issues their brothers may be too young to handle. If someone learns a new word he is afraid is inappropriate, or sees a headline about an adult subject, I tell him to ask Dad about it on their next walk. If I had any daughters, I could take a similar role with them. Sometimes it's a delicate balance to let the child lead the conversation (so that you aren't telling him more than he needs to know), while keeping him from wasting the time talking about trivialities.

Fathers should teach their choleric sons how to control their anger, feel and show compassion, respect women and the vulnerable, and submit to God's will. A father of any temperament may himself struggle in these areas. He and his child, especially if they are both choleric, can support and encourage each other. A choleric father can also guide children of both sexes towards worthwhile leadership opportunities and projects.

Studies show that girls tend to relate to potential spouses similarly to the way they related to their fathers. A choleric woman will need a husband who can accept her strong character. Since men in general tend to talk less than women, a father can be an excellent example of what it means to be a good listener. He can also teach her that being choleric does not mean being unwomanly. He can show her that he loves and cherishes her as a female, even while they do physical activities together. The father of a choleric daughter should be prepared to let her tell him all her concerns without criticizing her for talking too much. If her father accepts and supports her, she will more likely have the self-confidence to look for a supportive mate. She will also feel more comfortable with herself and her role in the world.

A sanguine father can help his choleric child learn to have fun without always having to win. His attitude towards favorite sports teams that lose and bad calls by referees teaches more than good sportsmanship. It teaches the child how to treat those with whom he disagrees—even his enemies. A phlegmatic father can demonstrate the importance of relationships, reminding his child to love people more than projects. A melancholic father can help him learn to pay more attention to the details that will help him succeed as a leader and a Christian.

Pope St. John Paul II wrote about the role of fathers:

> In revealing and in reliving on earth the very fatherhood of God, a man is called upon to ensure the harmonious and united development of all the members of the family: he will perform this task by exercising generous responsibility for the life conceived under the heart of the mother, by a more solicitous commitment to education, a task he shares with his wife, by work which is never a cause of division in the family but promotes its unity and stability, and by means of the witness he gives of an adult Christian life which effectively introduces the children into the living experience of Christ and the Church.[23]

Modeling Spiritual Growth

Two parenting skills will help you immensely as you work with your choleric child. They are modeling and good communication skills, with an emphasis on defusing power struggles. I will address communication, along with the issue of punishment and reward systems, in chapter 5. First, I'd like to talk about modeling.

---

[23] *Familiaris consortio*, no. 25.

When I first began blogging at Contemplative Homeschool, I intended to share my prayer-focused homeschooling method with the world. I quickly realized that parents could not teach their children about prayer if they were not prayerful themselves. My aim shifted to teaching adults how to grow in their faith so that they could pass this knowledge on to their children.

One of the most powerful ways of modifying your child's behavior is modeling—that is, practicing—the behavior you want to see in him. As author Mary Sheedy Kurcinka says, pre-teens want to be like their parents.[24] Your young children will try to copy you.

Since we implemented temperament studies in our home, I have found it much easier to relate to and correct my choleric child without it turning into an argument. Why is this? First, I have modeled being vulnerable. Not only does he know his own temperament and his brothers', he also knows mine. When I am struggling with my temperamental tendencies, I say so openly. My kids hear me say things such as, "My phlegmatic side really needs to be uninterrupted for a while." They know that when I am pressed to make a quick answer about whether they can do something, I am liable to say *no*. If I have time to think about it without being pestered, I might say *yes*. I tell them when little things are bothering me, warning them that I need some space so that I don't experience the slow build of melancholic anger that can rise beyond my control. When I yell at them, I later apologize. If I think I have made a mistake in disciplining them, I let them know. But I do all this of my own volition. If my choleric child pushes me to apologize, I will refuse. If he waits for me to have time for reflection, I will realize my error and say so. I mentor openness with my temperament, and my choleric child follows my example.

---

[24] Mary Sheedy Kurcinka, *Kids, Parents, and Power Struggles*, (New York: Harper Collins, 2000), 58.

Parents of other temperaments will, of course, have different areas to work on in their own lives, but they too can model being open and striving to overcome their natural weaknesses.

In your temperament studies, it is not you against your child. You can both be dispassionate. You can discuss problems rationally. You are a team working together. And there is nothing a choleric likes better than to know someone is on his team! Yes, it is his team, not yours. He benefits. He aims at becoming the best he can be. And though you are a coach, he is the star player. He is in control. Only he can make the decision to change. Sometimes when you make suggestions, he may reject them. Don't insist. Instead, ask if he can think of a better way to achieve the same end.

Here is something that will really encourage you as you work with your choleric child: his determination. More than any other characteristic, this is what makes cholerics great achievers. If he wants to control his temperament, he will find a way to do it. Nothing will hold him back. He may plow far ahead of your plans for him and you can watch in amazement.

Modeling is more important for your child's spiritual life than in any other area. Think about it. Teaching the faith goes beyond teaching the facts and dates of history, which may seldom impact your child's life. Being Catholic is not just for the classroom. It impacts every moment of our lives.

For too long parents have let Catholic school teachers or religious education instructors take all the responsibility for teaching kids the faith. "Religion" has been just another class to take, having little more significance for kids' lives than their science projects do. No wonder so many youth disengage from the faith after Confirmation! They feel like they have graduated from religious education. They "know" everything they need to for making an adult commitment to the faith. Done.

The Christian faith is not just an academic subject, and you don't want your children to think of it as one. Although it's vitally important to know about the faith, knowledge is just the beginning. The Catechism tells us we were made to know, love, and serve God. Notice, it doesn't say *know the faith*, but *know God*. We learn the faith in order to have an intimate relationship with God through Jesus Christ. The Church teaches us how. Then we must practice it.

Even school subjects must be practiced to be learned. What if you taught your child physical education by reading a book about sports? Would he ever become an athlete? Would he even truly understand how to play the games? Or what if you taught art by lecturing about color theory, but never opened a box a crayons? Not much chance of rearing an artist that way, is there? Nor is there much chance of raising a saint if the faith remains something to study, rather than to live.

Pope St. John Paul II wrote:

> For Christian parents the mission to educate, a mission rooted, as we have said, in their participation in God's creating activity, has a new specific source in the sacrament of marriage, which consecrates them for the strictly Christian education of their children: that is to say, it calls upon them to share in the very authority and love of God the Father and Christ the Shepherd, and in the motherly love of the Church, and it enriches them with wisdom, counsel, fortitude and all the other gifts of the Holy Spirit in order to help the children in their growth as human beings and as Christians.[25]

Jesus said, "Let the little children come to me, and do not hinder them."[26] Your child is naturally (and supernaturally since Baptism) designed to seek God. If his hunger for spiritual things is not satisfied in the Church, he will look for satisfaction elsewhere. Not hin-

---

[25] *Familiaris consortio,* no. 38.
[26] Mt 19:4.

dering him does not just mean moving out of his way. It means showing him the way. It means bringing him to Jesus. This is your God-given responsibility, no matter how your children learn their academic subjects or if they attend religious education classes. You are your child's first—and most important—teacher of the faith.

Catholic school teachers or religious educators can't give your child everything he needs to become intimate with Christ, because they don't live with your child. They are not well situated to show him how to behave when his plans fall through, when he is sick, or angry, or in a crisis. *But you are.*

Your choleric child will be the first to spy a hypocrite in a crowd. He demands authenticity. If you do not live your faith, he may conclude that you don't believe it, or that it is unworthy of belief.

Now, you may be discouraged, thinking, *But I'm so imperfect! I sin all the time.* Well, of course. You are human. God knows this better than you do. He has provided for it. You can use your weaknesses to your child's advantage.

You have the opportunity to demonstrate to your child that Original Sin exists. Yes, everyone in your family—and in the human race—is fallen. You are all tempted. You all sin. You also have the opportunity to demonstrate God's mercy and grace. When you sin against a family member, acknowledge it. Don't neglect to tell your child you are sorry when you discipline him too harshly or yell instead of teach. Forgive him when he sins against you or other family members. Don't hold a grudge. Don't prejudge him. Go to confession often, and take him with you once he reaches the age of reason. End every night by hugging him and saying, "I love you"—no matter how old he is, no matter what he has done.

Again, parents of different temperaments will find different aspects of this challenging, but it's too important for your family's well-being for you to shrug off your responsibility. If you want to help your child curb the negative aspects of his temperament, begin by curbing yours.

If your spouse is better at being open and vulnerable than you, consider letting him be the primary teacher about temperaments and spiritual growth.

Pray every day. Pray morning prayer with your kids at home-school or on the weekends. Pray before every meal, even in public. Teach your child to make the Sign of the Cross slowly and reverent-ly. Don't rush through the words, and don't allow him to do so ei-ther. Pray the Rosary with the whole family, at least now and then. Pray briefly as a family before bed. Set aside a specific time and place daily to pray mental prayer, talking to God from the heart, for a minimum of fifteen minutes. Make it your top priority. Be willing to give up everything before missing your intimate time alone with the Lord, and make sure your child knows about it. If you can commit to Eucharistic Adoration once a week, do so. If you can't, don't let it bother you. God still hears you at home.

Attend Mass every Sunday and Holy Day of Obligation. If you homeschool, try to work some extra Mass times into your schedule. Don't overwhelm yourself by thinking you need to go every day if you have an infant or toddler. Just do what you can. My youngest just turned four. Since last school year, we have been attending Mass with other homeschoolers one Friday a month, with breakfast at McDonald's afterward. Next year I hope to start going more often.

Be active in your parish or diocese as your family life permits. Do you have a gift you can share? Can you sing in the choir, lector, or help with funeral lunches? If you have little ones and can't take on a new commitment, maybe you could donate flowers from your gar-den to decorate the sanctuary or be a member of the prayer chain. You could also volunteer at a local crisis pregnancy center, or donate to the food bank regularly.

Talk about the faith as a family. On Sunday evenings, discuss the Mass readings and homily around the dinner table, beginning with the youngest family member who can talk. Our preschooler's usual contribution is recalling what color vestments the priest wore. Discuss current events in light of the faith.

Treat your spouse with love and respect. Never criticize him publicly, and absolutely never criticize him to your children. Make your spouse second only to God in your life. Show your child what a Christian marriage should look like.

If all this sounds like a lot, remember that you don't have to be perfect to be a good role model. You just have to be striving to grow closer to Christ. Your willingness to be vulnerable, to admit your mistakes, can be as valuable to your child as the elusive moral perfection.

CHAPTER 5

Communicating with Your Choleric Child

For some parents, the hardest part of parenting your choleric child may be communicating in a way that is both respectful and will get results. He can learn more effective communication skills from you, so that his determination, enthusiasm, or anger don't end in yelling, name-calling, or bullying others.

As part of good communication, your choleric needs to learn to openly express his love. I can be rather undemonstrative, and I wanted to make sure I told my children I loved them often. So I made it a habit to hug and kiss each child and say "Goodnight, I love you" every night after prayer. So far, no one has refused the signs of affection. My husband and I also have the custom of saying "I love you" to each other and each child when we get up in the morning, leave or return home, talk to one another on the phone, and even after we pray together. We also say "thank you" to each other for doing duties such as making dinner, taking out the garbage, or cleaning up a spill. Our choleric and all our children effortlessly do the same. This is our family's normal.

What about more general communication skills? How can those affect your ability to be your child's spiritual director?

Parenting experts agree that lecturing is seldom effective. Catholic psychologist and parenting specialist Dr. Ray Guerendi says that successful parents "talk less to be heard more."[27] The longer you talk, the less your kids will listen. You will find this to be particularly true of your choleric. He looks for the big picture and hurries over details. He grasps ideas quickly. Chances are, after your first sentence or two, he will change the subject or pick up a toy and pay more attention to it than to you. Amazingly, even the half of his mind that is listening to you may hear enough for him to act on what you say. But he still needs to learn how to be more respectful in his listening.

Instead of lecturing, try asking questions. "This is the third time this week you have broken something that belonged to one of your siblings. How do you suggest we change this pattern?" He may start by defending himself or blaming others. If he does, you could say, "But I want to know what you are going to do differently." Keep pressing this in a non-threatening way until he answers. After he has come up with some ideas and is not on the defensive, ask, "What are we going to do about this latest toy you broke? How will you make it up to your brother?"

Once again you are making him a partner. You are letting him be in control of the situation, finding his own solution. Just make sure it's one you can agree to!

Control and Power Struggles

Spiritual growth is in large part a process of surrendering to God. Each temperament has a primary fault, and each struggles with this

---

[27] Dr. Ray Guerendi and David Eich, *Back to the Family: Proven Advice on Building a Stronger, Healthier, Happier Family*, (New York: Simon and Schuster, 1991), 134.

surrender in a particular way. Each has a basic fear that he must overcome with the help of grace if he is to be a saint.

The choleric's greatest fear is losing control.[28] He will do whatever he can to remain in control of the situation. He has an agenda in every conversation and activity. If that agenda is threatened, he'll react strongly and at once. Keep in mind that this is a neutral characteristic in itself. While it can lead to the choleric's thinking that only his ideas matter, it can also make him a strong leader. He doesn't easily get distracted by trivialities or discouraged by failures. But it can lead to power struggles as well.

If a choleric is playing checkers with a sibling and you tell him it's time to set the table, he might refuse, complain, or argue. It's not that he minds the job itself, but that he wants to finish his game. Reminding him five minutes ahead that play time is almost finished can help him to change his agenda—at least until the table is set.

When arguing or debating, the choleric will want the last word. If you cannot agree with him or compromise with him, Art and Laraine Bennett suggest you try to find something in his argument to praise.[29] You could say, for example, "Although we disagree, you had some really good ideas." You could also point out that he has been right many times, just not in this case, or that you appreciated his calm, mature way of arguing.[30]

Allow him to debate you as long as he can do so respectfully. You should not punish him for mere disagreement, but he must distinguish it from backtalk. On your part, try to argue with him logically, setting emotion aside. If he is right, graciously tell him so. This will be harder for some parents than for others.

The choleric parent may be able to debate his choleric child in a dispassionate manner. He will not be bothered by his child's intensi-

---

[28] Littauer, 206.
[29] Bennetts, 57.
[30] Kurcinka, 88.

ty or easily hurt by his word choices. If you are this parent, enjoy helping your child refine his arguments while focusing on facts.

The sanguine parent may be surprised at his child's tenacity in arguing. If you are a sanguine parent, suggest a fun activity to do together once you have heard your child out. This might help him move on.

The melancholic parent is likely to have his anger build slowly in discussions with the choleric child. If you are melancholic, you can usually deal easily with the first disagreement or instance of backtalk, but by the third or fourth you may be ready to explode. Your challenge is to deal with any disagreements immediately so that they don't escalate into more than an academic discussion. The melancholic, even as an adult, has tender feelings.

What if your emotions are running too high during an argument, or you're an introvert who has a hard time making quick decisions? Don't be afraid to tell your child you need some space and time to think about what he has said. The phlegmatic parent often requires this to maintain the even temper he is known for. If you are a phlegmatic parent, you could say, "If you let me think about this for fifteen minutes in complete silence and solitude—absolutely no interruptions, understand—then I will try to make a reasonable decision." Emphasize that whatever decision you do make will be final, because you are the parent. If you come back with a decision he does not like, remind him that the discussion is now over. You have already heard his arguments. If he wants to have adult-level discussions with you in the future, he must agree not to push you once you have made your decision. You might also consider limiting the number of times in a day he can debate you so that he does not deplete all your energy.

Sometimes you may be so angry or otherwise emotional that you need to set aside making a decision until a later time. Fifteen minutes of thinking about a solution may just get you angrier, especially if you have melancholic tendencies. What you may need instead is something that will take your mind off the conflict and refresh you. Mary Sheedy Kurcinka suggests going for a walk, which will satisfy your body's need for action. After all, anger and anxiety are natural reactions that are meant to help you cope with emergencies. When adrenaline is pumping through your veins, a brisk walk might alleviate your stress. If you can't take a walk, try escaping in a book or taking a hot shower. Kurcinka even suggests washing dishes as a calming activity.[31] This last suggestion may work well for parents of young children who can't fully escape until after bedtime. Reading a calming story aloud to your children might also help.

Teach your child how to calm down as well. Start by telling him what you are doing to keep your emotions from getting out of control. For example: "I need to shelve this conversation so I can calm down. I'm going to take a quick walk around the block. I'll be back in five minutes, but I don't want you to bring this up again when I get back. We'll talk about it tomorrow." Next time you have an emotion-charged situation, you can suggest he do something to calm down too.

Discourage your child from going right from an emotional discussion to active play with his siblings or friends. He might get his anger out by being too rough and hurting someone. He can take a walk, ride his bike, shoot baskets alone, rearrange his dresser, or take a hot bath. My choleric son likes to write fiction at times like these. Although the choleric prefers not to spend much time alone, you don't want him to restart the discussion with a playmate. Encourage him to calm down for ten or fifteen minutes before he spends time with someone else.

---

[31] Kurcinka, 50.

Like all astute children, your choleric child may try to play one parent off against another in order to get his way. Do not allow him to do this. On trivial matters learn to back up your spouse, even if you would have made a different decision. Presenting a united front not only promotes unity, it shows respect for your spouse and his opinion—a respect you want your children to share. It also gives your child a sense of freedom to know that rules are firm. If you disagree with your spouse on some major aspect of child rearing or another important decision he has made, discuss these matters in private. Otherwise, the firmer spouse may find his decisions being undermined by a child who always seeks out the more lenient parent. Kurcinka says that when parents have another adult back up their decisions, children understand and remember them better.[32]

Since your choleric child is persistent, he expects you to be too. Do not tell him you are going to do anything that you don't plan to follow through on. He may take even the most casual statement of intent as a promise and be angry when you don't do as you said.

A Word about Reward Systems

Some parents are reluctant to motivate their children with rewards or punishments. Every couple must decide for themselves whether this is right for their family. Here is my take on the subject.

I have found that reward systems can be very effective *when combined with other means of discipline.* Offering a reward to a child for behavior you do not model yourself will probably not bring about a lasting change. But if you are modeling virtue and self-control and discussing temperament issues on a regular basis, rewards can work well, especially with your choleric child. The choleric is goal-oriented. He has activities he'd like to do more often and items he'd

---

[32] Kurcinka, 69.

like to buy. On many temperament issues, I give my children points every time they overcome the temptation we are working on. When they reach a certain threshold, they can cash in their points for extra movies, fun days at school, or trips to the park. One year we decided that if they overcame their habit of leaving lights on, we would reward them with take-out. Every day when no lights were left on, they earned $.25 toward their favorite Chinese dinner. To this day, three years later, they have maintained the habit of turning lights off.

This demonstrates the power of rewards. While your child is working toward a reward, he is forming new habits. The good behavior gradually becomes more natural to him. The challenge is to wean him from the reward at the right time, so that he keeps practicing the new behavior without it. On some issues, your choleric might balk at continuing to control his natural inclinations without a reward. Then you can point out the other benefits of the new behavior. Try to transfer his desire for a reward from privileges to better relationships with his siblings, less punishment for bad behavior, compliments from you and other adults, or more success in his school subjects. Show him as concretely as you can that his new habits benefit him. Emphasize how he is growing in his spiritual life by doing God's will more regularly. Ultimately, there is nothing wrong with desiring to benefit from good behavior. God desires that for us too. He rewards our obedience with an eternity in heaven (although we don't truly earn it). As we mature spiritually, we should begin acting out of pure love, but this takes years of spiritual growth, even for adults. If you let your child know that you do many difficult things without noticeable reward, this can plant a seed for the future. But don't lecture him about it, and don't expect him to be mature beyond his years.

CHAPTER 6

Helping the Choleric Learn Self-Control

E very person has a root sin (or two) that presents his biggest barrier to holiness. This root sin is usually related to his temperament. The choleric often struggles with anger, but even his anger is rooted in self-preservation. His root sin is pride. Your choleric child has high ideals. He has the strength, will, and talent to meet them. Humility is the virtue he needs most. He needs to acknowledge that he can only be holy with God's grace. He needs to recognize his weakness and sinfulness. He needs to learn that all his virtues and talents are gifts from God that he can easily take away. The choleric who has not learned humility is the most likely to become a tyrant.

He must learn to be respectful and charitable. He should cultivate compassion and patience.

Pride will be a lifelong struggle for the choleric. Prayer, especially meditating on the Gospels and on the meek but strong character of Jesus, may be his best tool for fighting it. Lesson Plan 1 focuses on learning humility from John the Baptist, a choleric saint. Lesson Plan 2, on servant leadership, can also help.

Many of the choleric's minor faults stem from his quick reaction time, his tendency to act or speak before thinking. In this chapter we will consider ways he can gain control over his emotions and pause before reacting.

The Choleric's Emotions

With a choleric child, model proper control of one's emotions. Kurcinka writes, "Kids who are emotionally smart are self-motivated, willing to cooperate, and able to get along with others."[33] The choleric is not naturally "emotionally smart." He might literally squirm if you ask him to talk about his feelings. He does not know how to manage his anger and may not even realize that he should. He freely expresses it, in keeping with his extroverted nature and quick reaction.

The choleric also tends to make light of others' feelings. Art and Laraine Bennett suggest a couple of reasons for this. First, he makes decisions based on logic, so he devalues the emotional life in general. This doesn't mean he is dispassionate. Past hurts, especially recent ones, can influence his judgment without his realizing it. He will probably vehemently deny it—but a discerning parent may be convinced it's the truth all the same. Second, he wants to maintain control, and exposing his emotions would lead to vulnerability. To help your choleric child feel safe to express himself, provide love and support and avoid quick judgments of his behavior.[34]

How can you begin to become your child's "emotion coach?" First, you have to be in control of your own emotions. Do you know which temperament you have and what problems with emotions that temperament tends toward? When your choleric child argues

---

[33] Kurcinka, *Power Struggles*, 5.
[34] Bennetts, 55.

with you, do you quickly lose control of yourself, ending up in a shouting match (choleric)? Or does your anger come more slowly, but finally burst out (melancholic)? Do you cry easily, without embarrassment (sanguine)? Or do you keep all your emotions hidden (phlegmatic)?

Kurcinka encourages parents to consciously ask themselves throughout the day, "How am I feeling at this moment?"[35] Begin voicing these feelings when appropriate. You don't want your choleric child to say, "Mom, you are always talking about your feelings!" But if he does, you can tell him you are doing it for his benefit. Once again, some parents will find this as difficult for themselves as it is for their child, but it is worth the effort for you both.

The choleric tenaciously hangs onto his impressions. When a choleric girl "accidentally" pulls the hair of a sister she was arguing with unsuccessfully fifteen minutes earlier, tell her you think she was really acting out of anger. The first few (hundred) times you do this, she may deny it, insisting it was an accident. For the choleric child "accident" often means "not consciously premeditated." "I didn't mean to hurt her," may really mean, "I wasn't thinking about how she would feel, I just needed to get my anger out."

Experts on anger say that it is often a response to loss of control.[36] When your child feels like a discussion, a chore, or a game is not going his way, he grasps for control wherever he can find it. He takes back control by yelling or making demands. He hides his fear and hurt so that others can't see his weaknesses.

The first step in learning to deal properly with your anger is recognizing when you are angry. If you ask your choleric child to think about what makes him angry, he may insist that he knows what triggers his anger and refuse to do as you ask. It is not easy to discern if

---

[35] *Power Struggles*, 46-47.
[36] Dr. Les Carter, *The Anger Trap*, (San Francisco: Jossey-Bass, 2003), 59-60.

this is true. The best way to help him recognize what triggers his anger may be through learning to recognize others' anger. See Lesson Plan 4 on empathy for ideas on how to go about this.

While he may express his anger by pronouncing judgment on his opponent, he will not realize that he was hurt. He deals exteriorly with the problem, but not interiorly. This unresolved hurt can turn into bitterness or hatred.[37]

Be careful of telling your spouse about the day's frustrations while your choleric child is within ear shot. Your child may revisit any disagreement with him you mention, starting to argue his point again. By talking about it you make him relive it. Try not to talk about these things until he has gone to bed.

Every temperament has its own way of manipulating others. Anger serves this purpose for the choleric. From his perspective, explosive anger or the threat of it helps him to maintain the control that he needs.[38] As a parent, you must show your child that there are better ways to get his needs met, ones that do not harm his relationships with others—or with God. If he believes he can succeed without anger, he will put in the effort to find better ways of relating.

Although he may seem to some parents to be unfeeling, the choleric does care a lot about other people, but this love can get buried underneath his outward shows of impatience and anger. He is not always aware of how his words come across to others. Thickskinned himself, he expects others to be the same. Fr. Jordan Aumann writes,

> Although they often have strong movements of irascibility and impatience in the face of problems, once they have conquered

---

[37] Bennetts, 55.
[38] Littauer, 22.

these movements they acquire a tenderness and sweetness of disposition that are noteworthy.[39]

This is the goal to work towards. You may not see much measurable progress in the years you have with your child. His reluctance to talk about his feelings often makes him reject any suggestions you give about controlling his anger. But if you can start the conversation with him, making him aware of his need to change, he will begin thinking about ways he can attack this problem. Give him time. Show him that *you* can be patient. Commend him for his insights. Do not nag or lecture him.

You might be dismayed as the parent of a sheltered choleric child to hear him using bad language. You don't allow those words in your home, nor does your child hang out with kids whose parents allow them. But he picks the words up here and there in books and movies or at school or elsewhere in public. With his noble ideals, he probably feels as horrified as you do to hear such language come out of his mouth. He might think he has committed a mortal sin. Swearing—at least before it has become a habit—is often a sign of anger. Your choleric gets mad, and instead of being violent, he curses. For some, this may even be a sign that he is striving to control more violent urges.

If this happens, ask your child what triggered his anger. Was he playing video games and stressed out about losing? Did he hit his head on the upper bunk of his bed? Did a friend cut him down or publicly embarrass him? Talk to him gently about the situation. Ask him how he can avoid a repeat of it. If you are understanding, rather than harsh, he may decide not to play video games as often, not to watch movies that contain bad language, or take other steps. Encourage him in making this mature decision. Gently remind him if

---

[39] Aumann, 2:7.

he goes back on it. He does not want to be controlled by his tongue any more than by another person—including you.

"Patience requires interior peace, sensitivity, and the ability to control our reactions."[40] All of this requires maturity.

The choleric can become depressed when he feels that he cannot control his life or circumstances. Psychologists say that depression is really turning one's anger against oneself. In some extreme circumstances, a choleric may take his own life as a means of seizing control.[41] We see this tendency in the push towards assisted suicide, which is often more about control than compassion. This is another reason why it's so vital for the choleric to learn to outwardly express his anger in appropriate ways. If he does not learn to do so, he may begin to mask his anger in public, especially if he has a secondary melancholic temperament. Then he is more likely to take his anger out on himself.

When a choleric feels depressed, don't pity him, or tell him God is trying to get his attention, or say that he is causing his own problems. You will only make him pull away. Instead, compliment him and show how much confidence you have in his ability.[42] Let him have more control where possible.

Thinking before Speaking

Mary Sheedy Kurcinka writes, "Extraverts 'think by talking.' To solve a problem or to reduce their stress, they need to talk with someone who will listen to them. Many times they don't even need a response from their listener. The opportunity to express themselves is all they need to work through their issues."[43]

---

[40] Bennetts, 181.
[41] Littauer, 197.
[42] Ibid.
[43] Kurcinka, *Spirited Child*, 63.

This need to speak can manifest itself in surprising (and to some parents, annoying) ways. Your choleric child asks you a question about current events. Before you have finished your first sentence, your child is stating his opinion with his normal (high) volume. You might accuse him of being disrespectful and an argument quickly follows.

What just happened? You thought he wanted you to instruct him. He really wanted to use you as a sounding board for his own reasoning. He was not trying to ignore you or talk over you. He was just trying to finish his thoughts. He might even contend that you interrupted him!

He needs to know that interrupting or talking over people—especially adults in authority over him—is unacceptable. When he acts this way, he should apologize, then politely ask you to repeat what you said, listening this time. Next time he asks a question like this, pose one of your own: "Do you really want me to answer, or are you just thinking out loud?" By asking this, you not only avoid a potential conflict, you also teach him to think about his desires and motives, a vital skill. This can be a first step for him in thinking before he speaks.

His speaking a thought almost as soon as it pops into his head will be a persistent challenge for you. When he says something disrespectful, insulting, or smart-alecky, focus first on the reason behind his words.

Was he trying to be funny? Sometimes a child genuinely doesn't understand how others will take his words. He might intend to make others laugh, but instead offends them. Often it's difficult to tell if he really did not understand how others would take his words or whether he just doesn't want to admit that he said something he shouldn't have. Let's say he says his sister looks like Anastasia from

Disney's *Cinderella*. Your daughter wails. You tell your son to go to his room. He protests, "It was only a joke!"

You ask, "Did you really think she would laugh? Anastasia is not a likable character. No one wants to be compared to her."

"But she has beautiful clothes," your son says. "I just meant that [my sister's] dress was beautiful."

Now you must decide whether to believe him or not. The choleric can think so quickly on his feet that he can supply a reasonable-sounding explanation for what was really meant as an insult or backtalk. Use your knowledge of your child to assess whether this was a deliberate act of unkindness. In most situations, he was probably just speaking without thinking first. The choleric rarely premeditates an insult or hurtful comment, because he doesn't reflect before he speaks at all. That lowers his culpability level, but it does not make it easier for him to have loving relationships with others.

Here is a mantra you can use with your child: *If you don't think before you speak, you'll have to think after you speak.* This means that when he insults a sibling he must go to his room and write at least five nice things (or whatever you think appropriate) about that person before coming out. If he talks to you disrespectfully, you might have him write five ways he could have made his point in a respectful manner.

Sometimes he may offend and hurt people through sheer thoughtlessness. He has a hard time putting himself in another's place. Since he tends to have thick skin, he may expect everyone else to also. Not minding physical contact, he may dismiss the idea that putting his face two inches from someone else's is going to elicit a negative reaction. In these cases, try having him write a paragraph about how the other person might have felt. If he protests that he has no idea or that his hearer is too sensitive, encourage him to think of it as a story. He could even make fictional characters to take the place of himself and the person he offended.

The choleric has a difficult time pausing between thinking and speaking. Everything he thinks tends to come out his mouth. But he can form habits of thinking first. Since he grasps situations so quickly, he should be able to feel, think, and then speak in the time it would take an introvert just to begin assessing what's going on.

Once you have taught him good listening skills, he can begin working on this next step in effective communication. If you are discussing something and he wants to talk, teach him to silently count to three before opening his mouth. At first he may concentrate completely on counting, and still say something he shouldn't or speak in a brusque manner. Use his desire for control to motivate him. Instruct him to think of doing battle with his tongue. Who will win, his tongue or himself? Can he control his tongue, or will his tongue control him? Remind him also that you will only listen to him if he is respectful. If he wants to be successful in life, he needs to speak in such a way that others will listen to him. If he wants them to support his cause or join his team, he must speak courteously and at the appropriate time.

Remember, if you are an extrovert who also has a problem thinking before speaking, you should practice this yourself too! Working on new habits together can be an excellent way to build your relationship and to show your child the importance of his relationship with God.

Talk to your choleric child about his bad speech habits at a time when he is not in an argument with you or others. For example, a few hours after you have had a disagreement, when you have both cooled down and you have good feelings for each other, return to the conversation. Don't dwell on the argument itself. This might just result in a new debate. Instead, gently point out how he could have used his tongue better. You might say, "I want to help you communicate your thoughts better, so that next time we disagree we don't get on each other's nerves so much. I don't want to talk about your arguments right now, but how you expressed them. When you interrupted me, it really set me on edge. Then I found it difficult to listen to you objectively. I couldn't really hear your point of view, because I was on the defensive. Next time, if you don't interrupt and you speak respectfully, I will try to consider your perspective."

If he tries to start the argument over, firmly say, "We are not talking about that right now. That discussion is over. We are talking about how we can communicate better in the future." If the discussion begins to get heated again, drop it for the time being.

After your next heated exchange—again, when you are cool—remind him of what you discussed about communication. If he begins to speak more calmly, commend him for it. If he stops interrupting, acknowledge it. Tell him you are proud to see how much he is maturing. Over time, he should gradually get better at making his three seconds of silence fruitful. Of course, if you have said that you would more easily consider his viewpoint if he speaks respectfully, you must uphold your side of the bargain. Be careful not to deny reasonable and respectful requests, or refuse to change your views, because of stubbornness, your own need for control, or past disagreements.

St. James the Greater was a choleric who came to value taming his tongue. A passage of his epistle gives instruction other cholerics should study:

> Let not many of you become teachers, my brethren, for you know that we who teach shall be judged with greater strictness. For we all make many mistakes, and if any one makes no mistakes in what he says he is a perfect man, able to bridle the whole body also. If we put bits into the mouths of horses that they may obey us, we guide their whole bodies. Look at the ships also; though they

are so great and are driven by strong winds, they are guided by a very small rudder wherever the will of the pilot directs. So the tongue is a little member and boasts of great things. How great a forest is set ablaze by a small fire!

And the tongue is a fire. The tongue is an unrighteous world among our members, staining the whole body, setting on fire the cycle of nature, and set on fire by hell. For every kind of beast and bird, of reptile and sea creature, can be tamed and has been tamed by humankind, but no human being can tame the tongue—a restless evil, full of deadly poison. With it we bless the Lord and Father, and with it we curse men, who are made in the likeness of God. From the same mouth come blessing and cursing. My brethren, this ought not to be so.[44]

St. Francis de Sales gives similar instructions, and says that the best way to avoid sins of the tongue is to avoid speaking too much:

Hence, in speech be brief and virtuous, brief and gentle, brief and simple, brief and charitable, brief and amiable.[45]

One way I have worked with all my children at being brief is teaching them to summarize. In homeschool, we often use narrations. I read a story or a passage of Scripture, and they tell it back to me, giving as many details as possible. Sometimes instead of a narration they give a six-point summary. You can teach your child to use this summary when he tells you about a movie, what happened at a play date, or any other conversation where he is wandering or provides too many details. Each point should be two sentences or less.

1. **What is the story about?** (This can be the introductory sentence, such as, "Katie told me something really funny today.")

---

[44] Jas 3:1-10.
[45] Source of quote unknown.

2. **What happened first?** (With some fiction and non-fiction stories, we add an extra step between one and two, asking, What question does this story answer? The summary then contains seven steps.)

3. **Then what happened?** (With stories we call this the "rising action.")

4. **What was the climax?** (This step should answer the question posed in the longer version of the summary, or be the punch line of a joke, et cetera.)

5. **What happened afterward?** (With stories we call this the "falling action.")

6. **How did the story end?** ("They lived happily ever after," or, "I laughed so hard, I fell off my chair.")

For more ideas, see Lesson Plan 3 on thinking before speaking.

CHAPTER 7

Siblings and Loving One's Neighbor

G od gives us families to help us learn how to love others at close range. Your children help each other learn what loving one's neighbor really means. Siblings don't choose each other, but they can choose to be kind to each other. Siblings teach your child that he is not meant to stand alone in the world, that he needs others in order to grow closer to God. They give him experience relating to people of different temperaments and personalities in a safe environment. He can practice patience, compassion, self-sacrifice, and generosity within the family.

Hands-off parenting does not work when you have children besides your choleric. You will want to monitor his relationships with his siblings, especially younger ones or those with a phlegmatic or melancholic temperament. The choleric can be hard to resist. If he doesn't get his way through using logical arguments, he often turns to name-calling and insults, or even physical violence. Since he doesn't like to give up in the face of opposition, he can keep pressuring a sibling to change his mind. A dutiful melancholic sibling might feel obligated to please his brother or sister, but later be resentful.

The choleric easily takes advantage of people with milder temperaments. He is so highly focused on his goals and interests that he can trivialize others' desires. He has a hard time seeing beyond the work that needs to get done to the feelings of those around him. If you have more than one choleric child, you have sibling rivalry on steroids. Choleric siblings constantly try to one-up each other. Each wants to be the best and can feel threatened by someone else who challenges his claim to the title. As soon as you recognize that you have more than one choleric, try to help them find different interests. If the elder loves volleyball, put the younger in soccer or swimming. In other words, try to minimize the competition however you can. Divide chores between them too. Rather than having them work on the same task at the same time, assign one to wash the dishes and the other to dry. Have one clean the upstairs and the other the downstairs, and rejoice that each is trying to do a better and faster job than the other. But beware of having them clean the same room together. Conflict is almost inevitable.

Your choleric child could make all the game, movie, and other free-time choices unless you intervene. Try having your kids take turns choosing the night's entertainment. Or designate a day each week for each child to choose what toys they can get out, what treat they get after dinner, and so on. Each child will know his turn is only a few days away. Each will learn to acquiesce to others' choices and never have to argue for his preferences.

If your other children are introverts, getting their energy by spending time alone, your choleric child will need socializing opportunities outside the home, especially as he grows older. Since the choleric loves to move around, has boundless energy, and is often a skilled athlete, team sports are a good option for him. If you homeschool and don't have access to league sports, try park board sports or swimming lessons. Girls can take dance or gymnastics classes as well. Make regular play dates or frequent outings. Don't expect other family members to fill all the choleric's socializing needs. Dropping him off to spend a few hours with friends can give you all a needed break.

Blaming and Lying

The choleric hates to admit that he has done something wrong. Some parents of choleric children become seriously concerned with their child's habit of lying. You or your spouse may witness your child misbehaving and he insists he is innocent. Too bad you didn't take a movie proving he did what you accused him of! You may wonder if he can tell the difference between right and wrong. As his first confession approaches, you may question if he will be able to recount his sins. Can he admit he has any?

Try not to be overly distressed about this negative aspect of his temperament. Often he will admit his failings to you later, perhaps during your weekly temperament discussion. The more sympathetic and open you are in these sessions, the more likely he is to admit his failures to you, both during and outside of this time.

When under pressure, a choleric will rarely accept criticism. He will rarely admit that he is wrong when he argues or fights with another person. Doing so, he thinks, gives his opponent momentary control over him. Instead of telling the truth, he will blame the other person, the weather, or even his innocent parents.

Knowing that this is part of his temperament should relieve you. No need to wonder if your child needs to get counseling for being delusional. But that does not mean you can excuse bending the truth. Lying is not acceptable. An adult who refuses to admit his mistakes will only make problems for himself. Lying is one step away from cheating, which is a serious offense. Come to think of it, the choleric is often accused of cheating in games as well.

God is truth. Satan is the father of lies.[46] To become the holy person God designed him to be, your child must learn to accept the truth. He must learn to admit that he is fallible. His lying is usually tied to pride.

When you confront him with his behavior and he lies about it, I believe you should punish him more severely than if he told the truth. You can also encourage him to tell the truth by lightening his punishment when he readily admits he was wrong.

Lying can also harm sibling relationships. When two kids have hurt each other physically or verbally, it's difficult to know who is most at fault when a choleric is involved. You will get completely different stories from the two children. The choleric can almost always make his behavior sound reasonable. Rather than letting one put the blame on the other, if you cannot figure out who started it, consider punishing both. This may not be ideal, but since you are not omniscient and will often be out of the room when they misbehave, it may be the best you can do. It teaches both kids that blaming the other person will not get them off the hook.

I never allow the excuse, "He hit me first!" Violence is not acceptable, unless it is self-defense. Punching back someone who has already stopped punching you does not meet the requirements. That is not self-defense. It is revenge.

Sometimes you may have to send your choleric child to his room until he can admit his fault. Once his quick-to-react adrenaline has quieted down, he is more likely to accept responsibility. Remember not to lecture him about his bad behavior. Lectures may make him less likely to admit his fault to you next time. If he can save face relatively quickly, his admission will not be as painful to him. Accept his

---

[46] John 8:44.

apology, commend him for being honest, and move on. If you need to discuss the issue further, wait a day or two if possible, and make the discussion brief. Make sure you give him time to make his own suggestions about how he can change his behavior.

Here are some ways to help your child move beyond blaming:

- Don't over-discipline, lecture, or yell at him.
- Don't tell your friends and relatives about his misbehavior.
- Be understanding with his weaknesses.
- Be consistent with your rules.
- Be fair.

Sometimes your choleric blames others as a way to save face. If you can help him save face while still disciplining him when he needs it, he may be less likely to pretend he did nothing wrong. His sense of justice tells him that he deserves punishment. What he hates worst of all is being humiliated. Don't act as though he is less worthy of respect because he has committed a sin. Instead, invite him to repentance.

It's important to teach him the difference between excuses and reasons. Pride often underlies excuses. People make excuses when they don't want to be taken to task for their poor behavior. Allowing your choleric child to make excuses is allowing him to pretend he is something he is not—a victim of circumstances. Point out that adults (or "big kids," depending on your child's age) take responsibility for their actions. Does your child let circumstances control him, or is he in control of them? If he is in control, excuses have no place.

Reasons, on the other hand, are circumstances that truly are outside your child's control. He can learn to give reasons for both his own and others' behavior. Instead of insulting a sibling who offends him, he can try to understand why his sibling acted that way. He can begin to have empathy for others as he learns to distinguish between excuses and reasons in his own life.

Encouraging Leadership Skills

Your choleric child has natural leadership abilities that you will want to encourage and guide. How can you raise a successful leader? Nicole Fallon, assistant editor at *Business News Daily*, writes that leaders should know how to listen, have a vision for the future, and understand that they should look after more than their own interests.[47] We have already talked about teaching your child to listen. He will naturally have a vision for anything he is interested in. That leaves looking out for others' interests.

Servant leadership can begin with studying the life of Jesus. Read Gospel stories with your child that show how Jesus never quavered when others opposed the truth, but was always gentle with sinners, patient with the weak, loving, and affectionate. Lesson Plan 2 on servant leadership is an ongoing project in our house. It has brought great returns. I have found it is not a one-time lesson for the choleric, but something he must consciously think of daily.

Your temperament studies can also help him hone his leadership skills, as he learns to see the strengths of people different from himself. The Catholic Leadership Institute recommends the movie *Twelve Angry Men* as a demonstration of the four temperaments at work among jury members for a murder trial. Our family loved watching this film. We found that each of us admired the characters who shared our temperament, and were more critical of the others. For teens, this could provide fodder for an excellent discussion of

---

[47] "4 Tips for Teaching Leadership Skills," *Business News Daily*, *www.businessnewsdaily.com/5818-leadership-training.html* (January 24, 2014).

working with people of different temperaments to accomplish a common task.

Unfortunately, most leadership books for Christians were written by Protestants and may only confuse your Catholic child. (I am thinking particularly of *The Purpose-Driven Life* by Rick Warren). Catholic author Randy Hain has written several books for business-people, but I do not know of a good Catholic resource for raising your child to be a leader. I invite readers to share any resources you recommend by sending me an email.

The Works of Mercy

Your child will be eager to share whatever he loves with the world. If he loves the faith, he will usually share it fearlessly. He can become a leader in both the world and the Church.

One way a choleric of any age can begin impacting the world for Christ is by performing the corporal and spiritual works of mercy,[48] which are closely connected to servant leadership. The corporal works of mercy are

- Feed the hungry.
- Give drink to the thirsty.
- Clothe the naked.
- Shelter the homeless.
- Visit the sick.
- Visit the imprisoned (formerly "ransom the captive").
- Bury the dead.

---

[48] Bennetts, 109.

These are taken from a passage in the Gospels concerning the Last Judgment:

> When the Son of man comes in his glory, and all the angels with him, then he will sit on his glorious throne. Before him will be gathered all the nations, and he will separate them one from another as a shepherd separates the sheep from the goats, and he will place the sheep at his right hand, but the goats at the left. Then the King will say to those at his right hand, "Come, O blessed of my Father, inherit the kingdom prepared for you from the foundation of the world; for I was hungry and you gave me food, I was thirsty and you gave me drink, I was a stranger and you welcomed me, I was naked and you clothed me, I was sick and you visited me, I was in prison and you came to me."
>
> Then the righteous will answer him, "Lord, when did we see thee hungry and feed thee, or thirsty and give thee drink? And when did we see thee a stranger and welcome thee, or naked and clothe thee? And when did we see thee sick or in prison and visit thee?"
>
> And the King will answer them, "Truly, I say to you, as you did it to one of the least of these my brethren, you did it to me."
>
> Then he will say to those at his left hand, "Depart from me, you cursed, into the eternal fire prepared for the devil and his angels; for I was hungry and you gave me no food, I was thirsty and you gave me no drink, I was a stranger and you did not welcome me, naked and you did not clothe me, sick and in prison and you did not visit me."
>
> Then they also will answer, "Lord, when did we see thee hungry or thirsty or a stranger or naked or sick or in prison, and did not minister to thee?"
>
> Then he will answer them, "Truly, I say to you, as you did it not to one of the least of these, you did it not to me." And they will go away into eternal punishment, but the righteous into eternal life.[49]

---

[49] Mt 25:31-46.

The choleric "tend(s) to see love as good deeds done or ministry projects completed."[50] He will probably be eager to take up the corporal works of mercy. However, he won't be content doing a little bit here and there. He will want a cause to pursue. I have included a lesson plan on the corporal works of mercy in chapter 13. The spiritual works of mercy will pose more of a challenge for your choleric. They are

- Instruct the ignorant.
- Counsel the doubtful.
- Admonish sinners.
- Bear wrongs patiently.
- Forgive offenses willingly.
- Comfort the afflicted.
- Pray for the living and the dead.

Start with having him do the last of these. He will love knowing his prayers make a real difference for people on earth and in Purgatory. Learning to bear wrongs patiently and forgive offenses willingly will be lifelong struggles, as will comforting the afflicted. Your example, especially in your dealings with him, your spouse, and your other children, can help.

On the other hand, he must be taught not to be too harsh when he instructs the ignorant or admonishes sinners. Teach him that pride can cause the opposite effect he hopes to see. If he can learn to instruct and admonish without judging others, he can have a powerful influence for the Kingdom of God, since he is seldom afraid to say what he thinks. We need young men and women like this!

---

[50] Ed Vasicek, "Temperament Theory," *Highland Park Church*, *www.highlandpc.com/articles/temptheo.php*, (accessed April 12, 2015).

Instructing the ignorant can begin in the home. If you home-school, allow your choleric child to teach a sibling phonics, or drill another on math facts. Watch his level of patience and make sure you give him a break from his duties before he gets frustrated. When he is older, let him give oral reports and persuasive speeches, especially ones dealing with the faith.

Allow him to correct friends and neighbors who take the Lord's name in vain or slip into other sinful behavior. Tell him that doing so once or twice is enough. More than this and his friend might feel controlled. Then his words could have the opposite effect he wants. Share with him stories of times you have gently corrected others with a good result, times you were too afraid to speak up, or times you were too harsh and wasted a good opportunity. Teach him through your failures as well as your successes.

CHAPTER 8

Your Home and Catholic Culture

The atmosphere of your home will affect your child's spiritual life. As a choleric, he is outwardly focused. He notices sights, sounds, and smells. A quiet, peaceful home provides the perfect atmosphere for the prayerful life you want to foster in your child. This chapter explores some ways you can provide the optimal environment for your choleric child.

How can you bring Catholic culture into your home? At one time in history, the Catholic faith was the greatest power behind western culture. The world's finest artists, architects, musicians, and writers all came from a Catholic worldview. They painted cathedrals, composed Mass settings, built St. Peter's basilica, and wrote about heaven, hell, and Purgatory. Sadly, our secularized world now produces profane works and calls them art.

Your choleric child will not naturally care as much about beauty as a sanguine child would. He will probably not become a poet, as a melancholic child might. He can easily adopt the attitude that beauty is unnecessary, even frivolous. Who has time for it, when there is so much work to do? In chapter 9, I'll briefly touch on teaching the choleric art in the homeschool classroom. Here I want to consider art as part of authentic Christian culture.

Experiencing Transcendent Beauty

Beauty appeals to the imagination. It can move your child to a greater desire for and love of God. An appreciation for beauty distinguishes humans from lower animals. The beauty of a sunset does not move a dog. A line from a hymn cannot create longing in the heart of a rabbit.

> Created "in the image of God," man also expresses the truth of his relationship with God the Creator by the beauty of his artistic works. Indeed, art is a distinctively human form of expression; beyond the search for the necessities of life which is common to all living creatures, art is a freely given superabundance of the human being's inner riches. Arising from talent given by the Creator and from man's own effort, art is a form of practical wisdom, uniting knowledge and skill, to give form to the truth of reality in a language accessible to sight or hearing. To the extent that it is inspired by truth and love of beings, art bears a certain likeness to God's activity in what he has created. Like any other human activity, art is not an absolute end in itself, but is ordered to and ennobled by the ultimate end of man.[51]

Your choleric child does not just have an intellect and a will. He also has an imagination, given to him by God to be another way to lead him towards divine union. The imagination does not remain empty. It seeks material to feed upon. How many times has your choleric child talked endlessly about a movie he enjoyed or a novel he read? How often have his dreams influenced the next day's play?

As a young child, your choleric was probably as interested in experiencing or producing art as anyone else, but he may grow less

---

[51] CCC 2051.

interested in it over time. This initial interest shows his natural need to satisfy his imagination. If he does not satisfy it with beauty, he may fill it with video games or pop music. Later in this chapter I talk about regulating your child's use of mass media, but this is not enough. You must supply his imagination with an alternative.

The easiest way to do this is to fill your home with religious objects. Try to find works by the masters or truly great contemporary artists. Some cholerics will disdain kitschy religious statues or syrupy paintings. Spending more money on one or two truly beautiful objects for your living room or family room will benefit your child more than many inexpensive, gaudy works. A Bible with beautiful, rather than cartoonish, illustrations can also fill this role. Listening to hymns, especially during the Christmas and Easter seasons, provides a holy backdrop for your daily activities. You can also celebrate your child's feast days with traditional dishes or a special dessert. Supply him with high-quality books to read, both fiction and nonfiction. Use the book list in chapter 12 to help you.

The soul longs for beauty. The beatific vision—the vision of God—fulfills this longing. A choleric adult may miss out on many of the things that make life meaningful and suffering bearable, if he does not form the habit of taking account of beauty. He may not recognize what is missing. God did not create a solely utilitarian earth. He placed Adam and Eve in a garden. Make your home a reflection of that garden for the benefit of your whole family.

Regulating Mass Media

Filling your home with beautiful Catholic works is only one part of forming your choleric child's imagination. The other is regulating the number of secular impressions entering his imagination through his senses. This means keeping the TV off during meals and limiting the television, radio, and other media.

Mary Sheedy Kurcinka writes:

> Spirited kids tend to love watching television. [They] don't just watch Batman, they become Batman. Turn off the tube and you'll have a maniac tearing around the house.[52]

Your choleric child will get wound up when he watches action or adventure shows. He will imitate the fights, the sports games, the dancing, and the slapstick humor he sees on TV. Limit his exposure, unless you want a constant circus in your home. One choleric parent has told me that such wild behavior doesn't bother her unless it lasts all day. Introverted parents, on the other hand, can be exhausted and exasperated by rambunctious behavior very quickly. You don't want to stifle your child's need for movement and self-expression, but you must balance it against any need for peace and quiet you may have. There is also a difference between allowing for your child's natural energy and enthusiasm and letting him spend too much time in activities that give him an adrenaline rush. One part of helping your choleric child control his emotions is helping him avoid unnecessary activities that tend to spin those emotions out of control. Someday he will have to choose all his activities himself. Give him guidelines now to help him.

More importantly than watching his emotional balance, take care with the level of immorality he views on the screen. Although the choleric is not particularly prone to sins of the flesh, it is your duty to ensure he is not faced with too much information too soon.

An instruction for parents from the Diocese of La Crosse, Wisconsin, says of children who have not yet reached puberty:

---

[52] Mary Sheddy Kurcinka, *Raising Your Spirited Child*, (New York: HarperCollins, 1998), 119.

In this stage, parents are *recommended* to withhold sexually explicit information that may interrupt a child's right to innocence. Thus, you must monitor and limit the influence of mass media on your children as well as scrutinize what other external pressures may be present.[53]

Respect this time, which the Church calls the latency period.

My choleric son loves to watch NFL football. Sometimes the worst commercials are played during the game. Our rule is that a parent has to be on hand while he watches sports. At first we monitored the commercials for him, changing to public television or other channels at the first sign of anything offensive. After he turned twelve, he asked if he could begin monitoring the commercials himself. I still sat in the room with him, doing homeschool preparation or other paperwork, but he handled the controls. Eventually I was able to retire to my desk, which is in the next room but still in sight of the TV. He has proved responsible in this, but it will still be some time before I let him watch football completely unsupervised— mostly because there are some advertisements he does not yet understand, and I don't want him to "learn" these matters from TV. We still avoid watching most of the commercials during the Super Bowl, and completely forbid watching the Half Time Show.

Other than football, my children only watch educational programs on regular TV. We have a library of DVDs that they can watch on their own, and we sometimes check movies out of the library. Most of these are G-rated. Since my choleric is now in junior high, we sometimes let him stay up late to watch a movie with me that is too mature for his younger brothers. But we are saving anything PG-13 for his thirteenth birthday or beyond.

Obscene and profane language in movies can pose a problem for your choleric. If he hears a word too many times, it will get into his

---

[53] *Hey Parents—Teach Them About Real Love! Parent Handbook on Human Sexuality,*(2003), no. 5. Emphasis in original.

head—and you know by now what happens to a choleric's thoughts. They come out his mouth. Since he already has trouble controlling what he says in heated moments, don't give him a new, offensive vocabulary. Of course, this also means you need to control your own tongue. Your choleric may love playing video games. They'll get his adrenaline running. Watch out if a brother or sister makes noise and causes him to lose his concentration! He could also easily play for hours, hoping to beat his high score. Then he'll be all wound up afterward. Limit his exposure as best you can.

The Internet, smartphones, and other electronic devices pose similar challenges. Your choleric already has a tendency to downplay relationships. Don't let him spend too much time with machines. Carefully monitored use of the worldwide-web can help him with school work or hobbies at the appropriate age. But don't let him pressure you to give him responsibility he can't yet handle. Think twice, and then twice again, before buying him any electronic device for his own use. Ask yourself, *Does he really need this? Or am I giving in to pressure from him or from people outside our family?* Remember, he has his whole life to surf the web. He has a few short years as a child in your household. Cherish those years. Don't assume that what is good for adults is also good for children.

Do you know that every sensory stimulus creates a memory? In fact, therapists now use sensory stimulation to help strengthen the memories of Alzheimer's patients. Recall how a smell can transport you back to childhood, or how you can still recite car commercials you saw thirty years ago. Every memory in turn is a potential distraction from what is important in life. When people fill their minds with sights and sounds, distraction in prayer follows. Kids are particularly susceptible to this, because their memories are so vivid.

Electronic media provides sensory stimulation without calling for any physical response in the user. Your child's body is designed to react to stress by movement. Instead, while watching TV or working on his iPad, he absorbs the sensory stimuli while sitting (relatively) still. Many studies have shown that kids' heart and breathing rates increase, and their bodies act unsettled when they view violent or exciting video images.

> This rapid intensity, frequency and duration of visual and auditory stimulation results in a "hard wiring" of the child's sensory system for high speed, with subsequent devastating effects on a child's ability to imagine, attend and focus on academic tasks. Dr. Dimitri Christakis found that each hour of TV watched daily between the ages of birth and seven years equated to a 10% increase in attention problems by age seven.[54]

The American Academy of Pediatrics, anything but a conservative organization, says:

> Studies have shown that excessive media use can lead to attention problems, school difficulties, sleep and eating disorders, and obesity. In addition, the Internet and cell phones can provide platforms for illicit and risky behaviors.[55]

They recommend limiting children's use of all electronic media combined to two hours a day. Children under two, they say, should not be exposed to digital media or television at all.

It is much easier to limit media use from the start than to curtail overuse. And of course as your child enters his later teen years, you may decide that more media exposure is appropriate. Be very prayerful as you discern what is right for your child at various ages.

---

[54] Chris Rowan, OTR, "The Impact of Technology on Child Sensory and Motor Development," www.sensomotorische-integratie.nl/CrisRowan.pdf, (accessed April 12, 2015).
[55] "Media and Children," www.aap.org/en-us/advocacy-and-policy/aap-health-initiatives/Pages/Media-and-Children.aspx.

This is another area where you must lead by your example. If you are constantly texting, on the Internet, or in front of the TV, your children will likely behave the same way.

For nearly a century, great Catholic thinkers have cautioned against an overuse or abuse of mass media, including Edith Stein (St. Teresa Benedicta of the Cross), Marshall McLuhan, the Council Fathers of Vatican II, Pope St. John Paul II, Cardinal Avery Dulles, and Peter Kreeft. As a person grows in intimacy with God, one of the purifications he must submit to is purification of the memory. All images that don't lead him closer to Christ will have to go. This can be a long and painful process. Do your child a favor and shield him from filling his mind with useless or harmful memories. Help him to fill his memory instead with a beauty that will support him on his journey toward God.

CHAPTER 9

When Your Home is a Classroom

Before continuing with your child's spiritual life, I'd like to say a few words about teaching the choleric. I am including some general suggestions for homeschool parents and classroom teachers. If you are not in charge of your child's or others' education, feel free to skim or skip this chapter.

As you know by now, the choleric child is bursting with energy. He is often a kinesthetic (hands-on) learner. As a pure extrovert, he thinks through problems by talking about them. He speaks out in class without raising his hand. He rises from his seat when he is supposed to be quietly working, taps his pencil on his books, or doodles on his desk. He doesn't fit many people's notions of the model student.

Seeing this and the choleric child's angry outbursts, teachers and doctors may even say he has attention deficit hyperactivity disorder (ADHD). Mary Sheedy Kurcinka writes in *Raising Your Spirited Child* about the differences between strong temperaments and ADHD. Both cholerics and children with ADHD may be easily distracted by what goes on around them. But the choleric, with effort, can focus on tasks you give him. The child with ADHD tries to focus but cannot. He cannot filter out the extra stimuli that is vying for his attention.[56] Medication will not help the choleric. He just needs to learn how to put his energy, enthusiasm, and determination to good use.

In our homeschool, we have followed the suggestion of Charlotte Mason, limiting each subject to about fifteen minutes when children are young. This keeps a choleric child from getting bored and restless. It also helps you cut out the unnecessary extra instruction that he so despises. The challenge is to begin lengthening the time of each subject as the child grows older.

Persistence and a good attention span are the two characteristics that most help a child succeed on standardized tests—even more so than IQ.[57] Your choleric child will shine in these areas. His desire to beat the competition will also help him reach for the highest score possible. Encourage your teenager to study for the SAT or ACT exams and work towards specific scholarships. The College Board's College-Level Placement (CLEP) and Advanced Placement tests can also gain him college credit while in high school.

A choleric whizzes through his assignments, finishing what you intended to be an hour-long assignment in fifteen minutes. Surprisingly, he usually does a good job on it too. Always have extra work on hand that he can do when he has finished what you really hoped to get done for the day, but avoid giving him busy work. He will likely complain and refuse to do it. He knows—perhaps better than you do—when an assignment is wasting his time.

The choleric loves to direct his own education. Traditional schools often fail him in this area. Too often his enthusiasm for a subject is held back and he is left bored. He begins to dislike school and loses all taste for learning new things. In homeschool, on the

[56] Kurcinka, *Spirited Child*, 34.
[57] William B. Carey, M.D. and Martha M. Jablow, *Understanding Your Child's Temperament,* (New York: Macmillan, 1997), 148-9.

other hand, you can work with your choleric child to choose subjects that both interest him and meet your goals.

I usually let my choleric child choose what we should study for science each year. Instead of following a writing program with textbooks and worksheets, I let him write stories of his choosing. Then we read the stories aloud and I critique them for grammar and writing style. This year (grade seven) he wrote a ninety-page story about a war between sharks and eels. It was a huge improvement over his first story, written two years ago. He works on his writing for fun throughout the day and even on weekends and during vacation, saving actual school time for other subjects.

By letting your choleric have an increasing say in his education, you are teaching him that learning is interesting and rewarding. You help him continue seeking knowledge and personal growth throughout his life.

Handwriting is one subject that may prove challenging for you. Usually a choleric has the ability to write neatly. When you are teaching him manuscript or cursive, he might form the letters nearly perfectly. But as soon as he writes a paper or takes a spelling test, you might find his writing nearly illegible. He does not see the importance of neatness. After all, he got the answers right, so who cares if his paper was a mess? He might even try to copy the illegible handwriting he associates with doctors or his favorite sports star. In addition, he sometimes doodles all over his paper in his need to keep moving. He needs to learn why good handwriting matters. Here, as in many areas, a logical argument that is demonstrably true could convince him to at least be neat in his school work.

As I mentioned in the previous chapter, choleric adults generally have little time for fine arts.[58] When he is young, your child will probably enjoy art class as much as anyone else. He may bring his

---

[58] LaHaye, 19.

persistence and determination to his drawing projects. Eventually you will find that he is drawing elaborate and accurate pictures, but only of subjects that already interest him. As he enters middle school or junior high, he may begin balking at doing art projects that you choose. Teach him to see what he enjoys with an artist's eye. Give him freedom to adapt the projects to his interests.

Instill art appreciation early as well. Encourage him to enter art contests at the local library or through Homeschool Legal Defense Association. If you live in a large metropolitan area, get a family membership to an art museum and make special outings there that will give him fond memories into adulthood. You can do similar activities with music and theater. Appreciation of the arts will round out your choleric's character, give him a connection with others, and perhaps even make him more sensitive to beauty.

Many cholerics grow up to be classic Renaissance men (or women), able to do almost anything. Try to deepen your child's proficiency in one or two subjects that he enjoys, so he can be a master, not just a jack of all trades.

Forming a Catholic Intellect

In our homeschool, the Bible, Church documents, and the writings of saints are the foundation of all our learning. I try to teach my children that the faith impacts every aspect of life, and everything they do should be an outgrowth of their relationship with God and his Church. Our studies are oriented towards preparation for supernatural (infused) contemplation.

Remember how at the beginning of this book we spoke of knowing, loving, and serving God? Knowledge comes first. We can only love what we know. We will only truly serve where we love. Your choleric child will relish learning about and defending what he believes.

Here is an example of how you can use his intellectual curiosity, love for logic, and determination to help him form lifelong habits. Choleric adults have difficulty resting on the Sabbath. You can train your child to relax on Sundays. Up to a certain age, he will appreciate the break from homework and chores. After all, those are usually someone else's idea, not his. Start fun family traditions on Sundays and he may maintain them into adulthood.

The Sabbath rest is the perfect subject for him to explore on his own through reading Scripture, the Catechism, and the teachings of the saints. If hard evidence convinces him of the need to rest on Sundays, he is more likely to make it a part of his agenda. You might even buy him a simple planner and encourage him to write in "rest" or "play" every Sunday after Mass. Or he could choose a leisure activity he would like to pursue and write it in at the proper time. I encourage my son to come up with interesting projects he reserves for Sunday afternoons. Then if he gets bored he isn't asking me what odd jobs he can do to earn money. If he forms this habit, not only will it help his spiritual growth, it will also help him maintain good physical health and a healthy family life.

He will also enjoy learning apologetics.[59] Teach him church history. Have him make charts comparing the early heresies, record dates on a timeline, and learn all the arguments to defend the faith against Protestantism, atheism, and moral relativism. Junior high school is a good time to begin digging deeply into the faith. I have found Peter Kreeft's books *Yes or No?* and *Back to Virtue* excellent for high school students. His *Socrates Meets...* series and many of his other books will also suit the choleric, who may devour them faster than you can buy them.

---

[59] Bennetts, 111.

After you have read together some of Kreeft's versions of Socratic dialogs, you can have your child write his own. Find an argument against the Catholic faith he is likely to come across and assign him to write a dialog of himself and an imaginary adversary. (Don't have him write about someone he knows, unless you want the book to be acted out in real life.) You could also do this with heresies throughout history: St. Paul meets Arianism, Pope St. John Paul II meets communism, et cetera.

Mere Christianity by C. S. Lewis is also a superior resource. After he has read it and you have discussed it together, see if he can begin to argue in a similar manner for specifically Catholic doctrines.

Encourage him to write letters to the editor and to your representatives at the state and federal levels, especially on Culture of Life matters. Many cholerics will do this routinely as adults. Teach him to write with clarity, civility, and humility, while not weakening his argument.

A younger child should spend lots of time reading the Bible, both during and outside of school hours. We have half a dozen different Bibles for school-aged children in our home, besides baby Bibles, books of individual Bible stories, and many versions of the Bible for adults. St. Jerome, the great Bible translator (and a choleric) wrote, "Ignorance of the Scriptures is ignorance of Christ." In chapters 10 and 11, we will see how Scripture can form the basis of a rich and ever-deepening prayer life for your child.

A choleric must be intellectually convinced of the truth of the faith in order to make it his own. Give him all the tools you can to help him be so.

CHAPTER 10

Prayer Development for the Choleric

Past popes have minced no words in speaking about the role of parents regarding prayer. For example, Pope St. John Paul II wrote:

> The concrete example and living witness of parents is fundamental and irreplaceable in educating their children to pray. Only by praying together with their children can a father and mother—exercising their royal priesthood—penetrate the innermost depths of their children's hearts and leave an impression that the future events in their lives will not be able to efface. Let us again listen to the appeal made by Paul VI to parents: "Mothers, do you teach your children the Christian prayers? Do you prepare them, in conjunction with the priests, for the sacraments that they receive when they are young: Confession, Communion and Confirmation? Do you encourage them when they are sick to think of Christ suffering, to invoke the aid of the Blessed Virgin and the saints? Do you say the family rosary together? And you, fathers, do you pray with your children, with the whole domestic community, at least sometimes? Your example of honesty in thought and action, joined to some common prayer, is a lesson for life, an act of worship of singular value. In this way you bring peace to

your homes: *Pax huic domui.* Remember, it is thus that you build up the Church."[60]

Prayer is at the heart of the spiritual life, no matter what age a person is. The most important prayer is the Holy Mass. Your faithful attendance at Mass on Sundays and Holy Days of Obligation, as well as your active participation in the liturgy, show your child the importance of the Church's prayer. Study together the different parts of the Mass, the meaning of the words of the Creed, and some of the common Latin phrases used—even if you attend Mass in English.

Stages of Prayer Development

Saints Teresa of Avila and John of the Cross are Doctors of the Church regarding prayer. Teresa's masterpiece on prayer, *Interior Castle*, provides the foundation for the Catholic understanding of stages of prayer. Since we are speaking about children, we don't need to concern ourselves with contemplative prayer here. Contemplative prayer is a gift God gives to those who have made a great deal of progress in their spiritual lives. But we should understand the two types of prayer that we can prayer with ordinary grace. They are vocal and mental prayer.

Vocal prayer uses words composed by someone else. The Our Father, Hail Mary, and Table Blessing are three of the first prayers children learn. Unfortunately, most instruction in prayer stops here. Many people teach their children to recite memorized prayers, but not what it means *to pray.*

Did you know that the Rosary is meant to be a means of meditating on the life of Christ? Although this may seem obvious to you, it is not obvious to children. If they try to focus on God during the

---

[60] *Familiaris consortio,* no. 60.

Rosary, they will probably focus on thinking about the words of the prayers, rather than the mysteries. The Rosary is the perfect way to teach children to begin meditating on the life of Christ. The Rosary prayed well easily moves into mental prayer.

What is mental prayer? Mental prayer is communicating with God from the heart. It can take many forms, from a simple, "Thank you, Jesus," when something goes well to sitting silently in God's presence.

Of all the different types of mental prayer, meditation on Sacred Scripture holds a special place.

> Meditation engages thought, imagination, emotion, and desire. This mobilization of faculties is necessary in order to deepen our convictions of faith, prompt the conversion of our heart, and strengthen our will to follow Christ. Christian prayer tries above all to meditate on the mysteries of Christ, as in *lectio divina* or the rosary. This form of prayerful reflection is of great value.[61]

In other words, meditating on Scripture teaches your child about Christ, while inspiring him to love and follow Christ. It engages his whole soul. The Catechism speaks powerfully about children and prayer:

> The catechesis of children... aims at teaching them to meditate on the Word of God in personal prayer, practicing it in liturgical prayer, and internalizing it all in order to bear fruit in a new life.[62]

Cholerics and Mental Prayer

Some experts believe that the choleric can become a contemplative with relative ease.[63] I do not mean that he will live a quiet, secluded

---

[61] CCC 2708.
[62] CCC 2688.
[63] Hock, 2:3.

life. That is obviously against his natural impulses (although some of the world's most famous monks have been cholerics). Rather, I mean that he can reach an advanced stage of intimacy with God in prayer. His determination helps him set aside distractions during prayer. He has great powers of concentration. However, each temperament can be distracted in prayer in its own way. For the choleric, his agenda sometimes distracts him. As an adult, this means work projects and apostolates occupy his mind. For a child, it may be school, sports, events he is planning, or a project he's developing. Teach your high-school-aged child to name all his projects at the beginning of his prayer time, surrendering each to God. He can say something like this: "Lord, I lay at your feet my history paper, my birthday party, and my volleyball game. I surrender them to your providence. Help me to trust you to take care of them while I spend this time focused on you." He may also benefit from keeping a notebook beside him during prayer. When an idea distracts him, he can write it down to review later, then return to prayer. Or if he does not want to write it down, he can make a mental note of it, trusting God to remind him of it later.

Since the choleric tends to brush aside emotions, he does not run away from difficulties in prayer. He won't expect to have consolations or be disappointed when he doesn't receive them. He can endure terrible suffering with heroism. As he grows up, he becomes used to working hard to reach his goals and he brings this strong work ethic to prayer.

This could also pose problems for his prayer development, however, just as in the rest of his spiritual life. The choleric has little sense of his shortcomings. He believes he can do anything if he makes up his mind to it. He is liable to make prayer an intellectual exercise—more of a Bible study than a conversation with Christ. And he is liable to give himself the credit for any advancing.

He won't like what he sees as touchy-feely prayers. He will often react negatively to charismatic methods of prayer.[64] Unless you introduce him to using his imagination in prayer as a child, he may find this also too "emotional" as an adult, thus missing out on one of the richest forms of prayer. There are many ways to introduce him to this tradition.

He will want to be shown how to practice mental prayer, then quickly move to doing it on his own. He grasps the essentials easily and doesn't want to keep going over them. He also feels freer to admit his faults silently to God than to talk with you about them. He wants to be the one in control of choosing a topic for meditation and for making resolutions. At the beginning, however, you might guide him towards texts to meditate upon, looking for passages that have practical applications and can give him a "plan of attack" for his life.

One of the first daily mental prayer practices you can teach your choleric child is an examination of conscience. Begin this as he prepares to receive the Sacrament of Reconciliation. Guide him through the Ten Commandments, having him ask himself whether he has sinned against any of them during the day. When he has practiced this with you a few times, encourage him to begin doing this every night in private. Remind him each evening, so he does not forget. You could even include a silent reflection on the commandments at the end of your family night prayers. That way, the whole family forms this habit together. Usually a child preparing for the sacraments will be eager to begin relating to God as a "big kid" and do his best to examine his conscience well.

While everyone should learn to examine his conscience regularly, it is especially important for the choleric. He can easily make excuses for himself or see only his strengths and (sometimes purposely) ignore his weaknesses. He needs to learn that humility is

---

[64] Bennetts, 228.

absolutely essential for spiritual growth. Recalling each evening how often he has failed God, he will begin to see that he really is not as strong as he thinks, that he needs grace and mercy like everyone else. This could lead to greater compassion for other sinners, a virtue that doesn't come naturally to him.

Ignatian Methods of Mental Prayer

St. Ignatius of Loyola was a Spanish knight in the sixteenth century. After repeated injuries, he was forced to give up his military career. He experienced a complete conversion and ended up founding the Society of Jesus—the Jesuit Order. Ignatius was a choleric who learned to put his temperament to use "for the greater glory of God" (the Jesuit motto).

Although by nature he had a keen mind, his conversion led him to go further than intellectual knowledge of the faith. He taught others to embrace the Gospel, bringing their deepest desires into agreement with God's will. Love, he said, is not a matter of feelings, but of action. His spirituality, explained in the classic guide *Spiritual Exercises*, keeps knowing, loving, and serving God in their perfect relationship with each other. He can help protect your choleric from being too cerebral in his prayer and his relationship with God.

Ignatius' Examen Prayer is a nightly reflection on the events of the day to determine how you used or misused God's grace. See the prayer pages in the following chapter for a version of the *Examen Prayer* that is suitable for young cholerics.

My Path to Heaven: A Young Person's Guide to the Faith by Geoffrey Bill, SJ (illustrated by Caryll Houselander) presents a child friendly version of the *Spiritual Exercises*. I recommend it for children ages ten to twelve. Your choleric child will probably want to pray through it on his own, rather than with you. It is a great starting place for learning an Ignatian form of meditation. You could begin by letting him read and pray with the book one day a week during homeschool time, or on a Saturday morning if he attends school outside the home.

After he finishes the book, talk to him about praying in the same manner on his own. Help him brainstorm a list of broad topics he can pray about, then allow him to choose one each day. At this point, he will probably still need you to help him set a time and place for prayer. Once a week, he can pray this way at the same time and place he used to read the book, gradually moving towards praying every day. Don't push him to pray this way too often or too long before he is ready. If you and other family members pray at the same time as he does, this will help him solidify the habit.

If he is practicing either Ignatian meditation or the more Carmelite method that follows, keep his nightly examination of conscience simple. As he matures into the mid-teen years, expose him to all these methods of mental prayer. Then let him choose one to practice daily. As an adult, he can then choose to add more meditation methods, or change from one to another as he sees fit.

A Carmelite Method

In our homeschool, we use the Golden Children's Bible as a basis for unit studies. Each unit ends with a guided meditation on the text. I created the meditations myself. I have posted a few of these on my blog. I have also included some in chapter 11 that I think are most helpful to the choleric. Start with the meditation on Mary and Martha in the section called *Learning to Use a Guided Meditation*. This example uses both a passage of Scripture and a religious painting for meditation. Discussing and reflecting on religious paintings can also be a starting point for meditation. Sometime in the future I hope to publish an entire book of the meditations I have made for my children.

We start doing these meditations in kindergarten. At that level, walk your child through every step of the prayer. As he becomes more practiced in it, give him greater freedom in the final section of the prayer, letting him converse with God in his own words instead of repeating mine or yours. I have included examples of both variations for the meditations in this book.

By ages ten to twelve, depending on the child, he should be able to begin creating his own meditations with a little help from you. If your child is in this age group or older and has never experienced a guided meditation, spend some time practicing that first. For the more experienced child or for a teen, encourage him to use his mind and imagination to read and ponder the Scriptures, then spend about five minutes praying about the passage.

In the next chapter, I provide a detailed example using the story of Jesus' baptism from Matthew's Gospel, beginning in the section called *Meditation on the Gospels*. A template for your child to use on his own follows it. Make as many copies as you need for your family's use. Walk your child through the example first. Then, about once a week, practice with him on another Scripture passage, using the template. After doing this a few times, give him the template and have him practice on his own. Review what he wrote and clarify any part he did not understand. It took my two oldest children, ages ten and twelve, a couple of times working on their own to fully understand the method.

Continue practicing the method this way once a week for three to five weeks. By then he will probably be ready for the next step. If he is not ready yet, let him continue as he has been doing until he is comfortable moving on.

The next step is to start simplifying the process, making it more of a prayer and less of a worksheet. He begins with the Sign of the Cross and an invocation to the Holy Spirit to guide him. Instead of writing down the sights and sounds in step 2, this time he simply imagines the scene for a few minutes. Then he continues on as before.

Once again, let him practice this for several weeks before moving on. Then he lists just one idea in step 3 and does step 4 in his head. He should try to make the entire prayer about ten minutes long, concentrating on the final step, which is the most important—conversing with God. If he runs out of things to say, he can return to the Scripture passage and find another idea to reflect (that is, meditate) on. He can also talk to God about other concerns. He should wait to write anything down until after he is done praying.

Finally, after about a year's practice with the method, he can extend his prayer time to fifteen minutes. Each subsequent year he should try to pray about five minutes longer, so that by the time he reaches adulthood, he is praying for thirty minutes at a time. The conversation (step 5) should be the part that is getting longer, not necessarily the reading or reflecting.

Remember, each child will advance at his own pace. Your choleric will probably want to skip some steps from the beginning. Use your discretion with this. You want to make sure he is not rushing through his prayer. He probably does not grasp the method as fully as he thinks. These details can be important in prayer.

CHAPTER 11

Meditations to Use with Your Child

This chapter contains the meditations and templates I wrote about in chapter 10. On the next page you'll find a version of St. Ignatius' Examen Prayer that the choleric can use for his nightly prayer, as a follow up to making his first confession. Read this through with your child the first time, then let him practice it on his own, using the guide until he has mastered the steps. I have focused on aspects of the Christian life that will appeal to cholerics in this version.

The other meditations follow it. Feel free to make copies of these prayers and templates for your family's use.

The Examen Prayer of St. Ignatius

1. Recall that we live in God's presence.

God created everything in the natural world. Without his love and attention, nothing would continue to exist. God surrounds us always with his power. He is the King of the Universe, and we are subjects of his kingdom. In your heart, bow before God's throne. Tell him you want to be his good servant and do his will.

2. Remember the day's blessings.

Think of three blessings that God gave you today. Thank him for them. Did you do well in school? Get along better than usual with friends or family? Have your favorite meal for dinner? Experience beautiful weather? Receive an answer to prayer?

3. Review your actions.

Think about the times today you were tempted to sin. When did you open your heart to God's grace and overcome temptation? Did you obey when you didn't feel like it? Did you work hard, even though you were tired? Did you bite your tongue, instead of insulting someone?

When did you give in to temptation today? Did you talk back to your parents? Did you tell a lie? Did you do your work so quickly that you didn't give it your best effort?

4. Ask for forgiveness.

Tell the Lord you are sorry for the sins you committed today. Ask for his grace to overcome temptation tomorrow. You can say this prayer, or pray in your own words:

"Lord Jesus, thank you for showing me the ways I disobeyed your will today. I am truly sorry for my sins. I desire to be your good servant. Please grant me the strength to resist temptation. Help me be determined to do your will, no matter how difficult it is."

5. Resolve to be strong in faith.

Tell God that you resolve to do better tomorrow, with his help. Be specific. You can pray something like this:

"King of the Universe, I resolve to use my strength to follow you. I resolve, with your grace, to fight temptation and resist the Devil. I promise to try harder tomorrow to … (add specific actions here). Amen."

Learning to Use a Guided Meditation

Christ in the House of Martha and Mary, attributed to Georg Friedrich Stettner.
See it in color at Wikimedia Commons.

1. **Read aloud to your child Luke 10:38-42, using your favorite children's Bible.**

2. **Study the painting above.**

    Ask your child to identify the people in the painting. Discuss the painting in this manner:

    1. Martha and Mary are both holding something. What do you think those objects are? What does each represent? *Mary is reading the Bible. This represents meditating on Sacred Scripture. Martha is holding a duck, symbolizing being busy with household tasks.*

    2. Who are the other people in the picture? *A servant and probably some of the apostles.*

3. What are they doing? *Cooking, sitting at the table waiting for dinner, talking together.*

4. How many people appear to have been listening to Jesus? *Only Mary does.*

5. Does Mary look disturbed by what Martha is saying? *No, she looks peaceful.*

6. Why do you think the artist filled the foreground/front of the picture with food? *To show how much work Martha had to do or had been doing.*

7. Do you think Martha was doing something important? *Yes, Jesus and his apostles needed to eat.*

8. What could she have done differently so she could sit and listen to Jesus too? *She could have made a simpler meal.*

3. **Remind your child of the Feeding of the Five Thousand.**

Summarize the story for him if necessary. Ask:

1. How much food did Jesus need to feed all those people? *Five loaves of bread and two fish.*

2. Do you think Martha needed to work all day to cook for Jesus? *Probably not, because he could have fed everyone miraculously, as he had done before.*

3. Why do you think Martha was working so hard? *She was probably trying to show Jesus how much she loved him by making him a great meal.*

4. **Only one thing is needed.**

Discuss:

1. What is the best way to show Jesus we love him? *Listening to him and spending time with him, as Mary did.*

2. How can we sit at Jesus' feet today? *Go to Mass, read the Bible, and pray.*

3. Jesus said only one thing was needed. What is this one thing? *Spending time with God.*

5. **Lead your child in prayer.**

Make the Sign of the Cross, then have your child close his eyes and picture the painting in his mind. This time, he is sitting at Jesus' feet in Mary's place.

For a child about age eight or older say: "Imagine what Jesus would say to you as you sat with him. What would you say back? Speak to Jesus now in your heart, just as you would speak if you were sitting at his feet." For a younger child, skip down to the final paragraph.

Sit in silence for a few minutes, with the length of time depending on your child's age. Stop before he gets too uncomfortable.

Then pray this prayer phrase by phrase, and let him repeat it (or read it with you for ages ten and older):

"Dear Jesus, I know you are with me, just as you were with Mary and Martha. You visit me in the Eucharist. You love me and watch over me at every moment. Thank you that we can speak to you just as Mary could. Help me always to listen to you. Teach me to pray to you from my heart every day. Never let me get too busy to spend time with you. I love you, Jesus. Be with me always. Amen."

More Guided Meditations for Cholerics

For each of the meditations that follow, read and discuss the Bible stories before using the prayer. Make sure your child understands the stories. Discuss any difficult words or concepts. Each has a variation for the younger child (Level 1) and for the child more experienced in meditative prayer (Level 2). Feel free to adapt the meditations to fit your child's interests and struggles. You read the first part of the prayer aloud, pausing where indicated. Then you read the second part, phrase by phrase, letting a young child repeat the prayer.

David and Goliath Prayer (1 Sam 17)

Close your eyes and imagine you are David. You stand facing the tallest and strongest man you have ever seen. Goliath towers over you by more than two feet. He is dressed in bronze armor, while you wear only your shepherd's clothes. You are naturally afraid, but you put your trust in God. You know God wants you to win this battle. You feel his courage surging through you as you fit a stone in your sling. [Pause]

Now imagine that your greatest enemy is within you. Due to Original Sin, part of you wants to be selfish, greedy, and angry. When you feel your enemy, your "inner bully," towering over you, you can trust God to help you win the battle. You can slay your desire to sin as David slew Goliath. [Pause]

[Level 1, to be repeated, phrase by phrase by your child.] Let us pray. Lord Jesus, when you were on earth, you fought against your enemy, the Devil, to bring us victory over sin. Help me to be your good soldier. When I am tired of fighting, or think I cannot win, give me the strength and courage to continue to fight well. Help me to overcome the world, the flesh, and the Devil. Amen.

[Level 2] In your own words, ask God to help you be strong and courageous like David when you are tempted to sin. [Pause for several seconds.] Amen.

Healing of the Paralytic Prayer (Mk 2:1-12)

Close your eyes and imagine you are a paralytic. You are lying on a mat. You cannot move your arms and legs. You have been this way for years. You would give anything to be able to get up and play, walk, or run! [Pause]

Now imagine you see Jesus bending over you. His face is full of love and mercy. He gently touches your forehead and says, "Get up, take your mat, and walk." [Pause]

[Level 2, added step in this one] Think about how you react (don't say it aloud). What do you say and do? [Pause]

[Both levels, repeat phrase by phrase.] Let us pray. Lord Jesus, thank you for your love and mercy. Thank you for doctors and medicine that heal me. I know you always hear my prayers when I ask for help. When I am sick or hurt, please make me well again, through natural means or through a miracle. You are our Divine Doctor, and I praise you. Amen.

Golden Calf Prayer (Ex 32)

Close your eyes and imagine you are at the foot of Mt. Sinai with all the Israelites. Moses has been on the mountain a long time. Some people are saying that he must be dead. They want to make idols to worship. You remember how the God of Israel saved you from the Egyptians. You shout, "No! The Lord is the one and only God. I will only worship him!" [Pause.]

Now imagine your friend invites you to a slumber party on Saturday night. You know that if you go, you will not make it to Sunday Mass. But all your friends will be there and you are tempted to join them. Then you think about God's commandment to honor the Sabbath. You choose to love God more than yourself, and to obey him even when you would rather do something else. You tell your friend you cannot go and let him know why. [Pause]

[Level 1] Let us pray. Father in heaven, I thank you for all your commandments, which teach me to do what is right. Help me to love you above all things, even my own desires. I want to love you with my whole heart, my whole mind, and my whole strength, so that I can be with you in heaven. Give me the grace to do this every day. Amen.

[Level 2] In your own words, speak to God in your heart. Tell him how determined you are to obey his commands. Ask him for help to always put him and his will first. [Pause for a few minutes.] Amen.

Jesus Raises a Dead Girl Prayer (Mk 5:21-43)

Imagine you are very sick. Lying on your bed at home, you are too weak to even open your eyes. You live in the Holy Land two thousand years ago. You cannot go to a hospital and the doctors cannot save you. You struggle for breath. You hear your mother crying. Then everything begins to fade. You can't hear your parents any more. You can't picture anything in your mind. Everything is dark and you are scared. [Pause]

Now imagine that in the darkness, you hear a voice. It breaks through loudly and clearly. It is loving and strong. "Child," it says, "arise." Immediately you take a deep breath. You open your eyes. Jesus is sitting beside your bed, holding your hand. Your room is filled with light. You sit up and throw your arms around him. You feel perfectly well. [Pause]

[Level 1] Dear Jesus, I know that you are always with me. Help me not to be scared of the dark, of sickness, or of death. Fill me with your peace. Hold my hand when I feel afraid. Amen.

[Level 2] In your heart, tell Jesus about your greatest fears. Ask him to be with you whenever you are afraid, when you feel like everything is dark. Ask him for peace and trust in him. [Pause for several minutes or as long as appropriate.] Amen.

Meditation on the Gospels

1. Read a small section of the Gospels.

First, choose one of the four Gospels to pray through from beginning to end. Then choose from it a passage of ten to twenty verses. For this example, we're using Mark 1:1-11. Read it silently and slowly.

2. Use your senses.

Record the sights, sounds, smells, et cetera, that you would encounter if you were present when this story took place. Brainstorm as many as you can think of. Here are a few for our example:

- John's camel-hair clothing
- the sound of running water
- crowd noise

3. Look for a lesson.

What can you learn from this passage? Look for insight into Jesus' character, instruction in the faith, or practical spiritual help. List at least two or three lessons. Here are some possibilities:

1. Before Jesus comes to us, we must prepare our hearts.
2. John considered himself unworthy to untie Jesus' sandals.
3. Jesus will baptize with the Holy Spirit.
4. God is Father, Son, and Holy Spirit.
5. The Father is pleased with Jesus.

4. What does this mean?

Circle one of the lessons from step 3 to focus on. What does it mean for you? How can you apply it to your life? Why does it matter?

We will use no. 1: Before Jesus comes to us, we must prepare our hearts.

How can you prepare the way for Jesus in your heart? *You can be ready to do whatever God asks of you.* Is God asking anything of you right now that you are resisting? Is he calling you to give up any sin or attachment that you don't want to let go of? Have you been resisting his grace in any way?

Since this step tends to be very personal, write down two or three questions like these you are asking yourself, rather than the answers to the questions (so you can share the meditation with your parents or teacher). Answer them in your mind.

5. Talk to God.

Talk to God about your reflections. Ask him to send the Holy Spirit to help you. If necessary, ask for forgiveness. Make resolutions and tell God what you intend to do.

Example:

> "Father in Heaven, I want to make my heart ready for your Son, Jesus, to come to me. Please send me your Spirit to give me strength. I know you are asking me to _____ and it's hard for me to do. Please forgive me for not obeying you recently. Change my heart so I am eager to obey you. I promise to use the grace that you are giving me to overcome temptation. Thank you for your aid. Amen."

For a larger version of the following template to print for family use, please join my email readers list at ContemplativeHomeschool.com

Meditation on the Gospel

Name_____ Date_____

1. Choose a passage of 10–20 verses _____

2. Use your senses.

Brainstorm the sights, sounds, smells, tastes, and (physical) feelings you might encounter if you were present when the story took place

_____

_____

_____

_____

3. Look for a lesson.

What can you learn from this passage? List three ideas that show insight into Jesus' character, instruction in the faith, or practical spiritual advice._____

_____

_____

_____

4. What does this mean?

Circle one of the lessons from number 3 to focus on. What does it mean for you? How can you apply it to your life? Why does it matter? Since this step tends to be very personal, write down two or three questions like these that you are asking yourself, rather than the answers to the questions (so you can share the meditation with your parents or teacher). _____

_____

_____

_____

5.Talk to God.

Talk to God about your reflections. Ask him to send the Holy Spirit to help you. If necessary, ask for forgiveness. Make resolutions and tell God what you intend to do.

CHAPTER 12

Checklists

Saints and Heroes for Your Child to Imitate

Please note that I am not recommending that your child imitate all aspects of the lives of the people here, only the positive ones! Problematic behavior from some of these famous people can generate great conversations with your choleric child. Starred names are included in the lesson plans section.

St. John the Baptist*

St. Paul the Apostle (choleric-melancholic)

St. James the Greater (son of Zebedee)

St. Cyril of Alexandria

St. Jerome

St. Basil the Great

St. Thomas Beckett (choleric-sanguine)

St. Ignatius Loyola

Judith

Deborah

St. Martha

St. Joan of Arc (choleric-melancholic)*

Alexander the Great

Harriet Tubman

Helen Keller

Winston Churchill

Margaret Thatcher

Mother Angelica

MaryJo Copeland (choleric-sanguine)

Choleric Book List

The following list is organized by virtue, then age group. *BOV* and *MC* refer to stories found in William Bennett's *Book of Virtues* and *The Moral Compass*. Starred items are included in the lesson plans in chapter 14.

Compassion and Forgiveness

All Ages

"The Lion and the Mouse" by Aesop *(BOV)*
The Good Samaritan (Lk 10:25-17)
"Diamonds and Toads" by Charles Perrault *(BOV)*
The King of the Golden River by John Ruskin
Joseph and his brothers (Genesis)

Primary Grades

Stella Luna by Janell Cannon
The Hundred Dresses by Eleanor Estes
Shoeshine Girl by Clyde Robert Bulla

Middle Grades

"Androcles and the Lion" by James Baldwin *(BOV)*
A Christmas Carol by Charles Dickens
"Where Love is, God is" by Leo Tolstoy *(BOV)*
"Count That Day Lost" by George Eliot *(BOV)*
"The Little Girl Who Dared" *(MC)*
Charlotte's Web by E. B. White
Alan and Naomi by Myron Levoy
Amistad: A Long Road to Freedom by Walter Dean Myers
Anson's Way by Gary D. Schmidt
The Witch of Blackbird Pond by Elizabeth George Speare

Junior High and Older

To Kill a Mockingbird by Harper Lee

Patience and Anger Management

All Ages
"The King and His Hawk" by James Baldwin *(BOV)*

Primary Grades
"Let Dogs Delight to Bark and Bite" by Isaac Watts *(BOV)*
When Sophie Gets Angry... Really, Really Angry by Molly Bang

Middle Grades
What to Do When Your Temper Flares: A Kid's Guide to Overcoming Problems with Anger by Dawn Huebner and Bonnie Matthews

Thinking before Acting or Speaking

All Ages
"Diamonds and Toads" by Charles Perrault *(BOV)*
"Our Lips and Ears" *(BOV)*
"The Frogs and the Well" by Aesop *(BOV)*

Junior High and Older
"George Washington's Rules of Civility" *(BOV)*

Humility

All Ages
"Our Lips and Ears" *(BOV)*
"The Fox and the Cat" *(MC)*
"The Gold Bread" *(MC)*
"Arachne" *(MC)*
Sarah, Plain and Tall by Patricia MacLachlan

Primary Grades
Moses: When Harriet Tubman Led Her People to Freedom by Carol Boston Weatherford
Better Than You by Trudy Ludwig

Middle Grades
"King Canute on the Seashore" by Clifton Johnson *(BOV)*
"Phaeton" by Thomas Bullfinch *(BOV)*

Beorn the Proud by Madeleine A. Polland

Junior High and Older
"Ozymandias" by Percy Bysshe Shelly *(BOV)*
Dombey and Son by Charles Dickens
Pride and Prejudice by Jane Austen

Respect and Obedience

All Ages
"Dr. Johnson and His Father" *(MC)*

Primary Grades
Bicycle Man by Alan Say
Story about Ping by Marjorie Flack
The Whipping Boy by Sid Fleischman

Being a Good Leader

All Ages
"The Hill" *(MC)*
The Boxcar Children by Gertrude Chandler Warren
Three Billy Goats Gruff by P.J. Asbjornsen, Illus. by Marcia Brown*

Middle Grades
Mother Teresa by Demi*
Molly Pitcher: Young Patriot by Augusta Stevenson
Nathan Hale: Revolutionary Hero by Loree Lough

Books with Choleric Main Characters

All Ages
Ramona the Pest and other Ramona Books by Beverly Cleary
The *Little House* books by Laura Ingalls Wilder (choleric-
    melancholic)
The Lion, the Witch, and the Wardrobe and *The Voyage of the Dawn
    Treader* by C. S. Lewis
Beauty and the Beast by Jan Brett

Primary Grades
Madeleine and series by Ludwig Bemelmans
Where the Wild Things Are by Maurice Sendak

Middle Grades and Older
Anne of Green Gables and series by L. M. Montgomery
Caddie Woodlawn by Carol Ryrie Brink
The Secret Garden by Frances Hodgson Burnett
The Book of Three and series by Lloyd Alexander
The Witch of Blackbird Pond by Elizabeth George Speare
Little Women, Jo's Boys, and *Little Men* by Louisa May Alcott

Bible Verses for the Choleric Child

In addition to the verses given in the following list for memorizing, some chapters and even whole books are especially good for cholerics to read and study. When it comes to the Gospels, some cholerics may be unable to relate to John's Gospel, considering it too emotion-based. "Cholerics often favor Mark's Gospel, because it is short, to the point, and informative."[65] Proverbs is filled with teaching on obedience, humility, and true versus false wisdom. Sirach is a similar piece of wisdom literature. Romans 12 speaks of humility, patience, love, and forgiveness. It and 1 Corinthians 13, the famous chapter on true love, provide perfect texts for cholerics to memorize. Philippians also provides an excellent study on humility and surrender. Choleric girls may enjoy reading the book of Judith, while choleric boys may enjoy the stories of the Maccabees.

Humility

If the prophet had commanded you to do some great thing, would you not have done it? How much rather, then, when he says to you, "Wash, and be clean?" (2 Kgs 5:13)

Trust in the LORD with all your heart, and lean not on your own understanding; In all your ways acknowledge Him, and He shall direct your paths. (Prv 3:5-6)

When pride comes, then comes disgrace; but wisdom is with the humble. (Prv 11:2)

He who conceals his transgressions will not prosper, but he who confesses and forsakes them will obtain mercy. (Prv 28:13)

If today you hear His voice, harden not your hearts. (Ps 25:7-8)

---

[65] Vasicek, "Temperament Theory."

Truly, I say to you, whoever does not receive the kingdom of God like a child shall not enter it. (Mk 10:15)

He must increase, but I must decrease. (Jn 3:30)

All have sinned and fall short of the glory of God. (Rom 3:23)

Abraham believed God, and it was credited to him as righteousness. (Gal 3:6)

For by grace you have been saved through faith; and this is not your own doing, it is the gift of God—not because of works, lest any man should boast. (Eph 2:8-9)

Do nothing from selfishness or conceit, but in humility count others better than yourselves. Let each of you look not only to his own interests, but also to the interests of others. (Phil 2:3-4)

Humble yourselves before the Lord and he will exalt you. (Jas 4:10)

Finally, all of you, have unity of spirit, sympathy, love for one another, a tender heart, and a humble mind. (1 Pet 3:8)

Compassion

I desire mercy, and not sacrifice. (Hos 6:6)

Blessed are the merciful, for they shall obtain mercy. (Mt 5:7)

Do unto others as you would have them do unto you. (Mt 7:20)

Rejoice with those who rejoice, and weep with those who weep. (Rom 12:15)

If your enemy is hungry, feed him; if he is thirsty, give him drink; for by so doing you will heap burning coals upon his head. (Rom 12:20)

Bear one another's burdens, and so fulfill the law of Christ. (Gal 6:2)

So then, as we have opportunity, let us do good to all men, and especially to those who are of the household of faith. (Gal 6:10)

Be kind to one another, tenderhearted, forgiving one another, as God in Christ forgave you. (Eph 4:32)

Do not neglect to show hospitality to strangers, for thereby some have entertained angels unawares. (Heb 13:2)

Servant Leadership

Open your mouth, judge righteously, maintain the rights of the poor and needy. (Prv 31:9)

Whoever receives this child in my name receives me. (Lk 8:48)

He who is faithful in a very little is faithful also in much; and he who is dishonest in a very little is dishonest also in much. (Lk 16:10)

So, whether you eat or drink, or whatever you do, do everything for the glory of God. (1 Cor 10:31)

Preach the word, be urgent in season and out of season, convince, rebuke, and exhort, be unfailing in patience and in teaching. (2 Tim 4:2)

Let no one despise your youth, but set the believers an example in speech and conduct, in love, in faith, in purity. (1 Tim 4:12)

Patience

He who is slow to anger has great understanding, but he who has a hasty temper exalts folly. (Prv 14:29)

We who are strong ought to bear with the failings of the weak. (Rom 15:1)

Be angry but do not sin; do not let the sun go down on your anger. (Eph 4:26)

Put on then, as God's chosen ones, holy and beloved, compassion, kindness, lowliness, meekness, and patience. (Col 3:12)

Let every man be quick to hear, slow to speak, slow to anger, for the anger of man does not work the righteousness of God. (Jas 1:19-20)

Who is wise and understanding among you? By his good life let him show his works in the meekness of wisdom. (Jas 3:13)

For what credit is it, if when you do wrong and are beaten for it, you take it patiently? But if when you do right and suffer for, it you take it patiently, you have God's approval. (1 Pet 2:20)

Respect and Obedience

All that the Lord has spoken we will do, and we will be obedient. (Ex 24:7)

Whoever honors his father will be gladdened by his own children, and when he prays he will be heard. (Sir 3:5)

A man's glory comes from honoring his father, and it is a disgrace for children not to respect their mother. (Sir 3:11)

Children, obey your parents in the Lord, for this is right. "Honor your father and mother" (this is the first commandment with a promise),"that it may be well with you and that you may live long on the earth." (Eph 6:1-3)

Obey your leaders and submit to them, for they watch on behalf of your souls, as those who will give account, that they may do this with joy, and not with groaning, for that would be unprofitable for you. (Heb 13:17)

Thinking before Speaking

Whoever belittles another lacks sense, but an intelligent person remains silent. (Prv 11:12)

No foul language should come out of your mouths, but only what is needed to build others up, so that it may benefit those who hear. (Eph 4:29)

Prayer

For where two or three are gathered in my name, there am I in the midst of them. (Mt 18:20)

Miscellaneous

The truth will set you free. (Jn 8:32)

Your adversary the devil prowls around like a roaring lion, seeking someone to devour. (1 Pet 5:8)

CHAPTER 13

Lesson Plans

The five lesson plans that follow are actually units or mini-units on a particular area of spiritual development for the choleric. Spread the different steps out over several days. Some, such as Lesson Plan 2, can become the focus of several weeks of temperament studies with your child. As always, feel free to adapt the lessons to your child's age, sex, and interests. You can also use these lessons with all your children together, or even with a small homeschool co-op.

Lesson Plan 1: First Steps in Humility

Ages: 8-14

Objective: The child will begin giving God glory for all his gifts.

Summary: Starting with St. John the Baptist, this lesson will focus on the fact that all strength and talent comes from God. You will read what Jesus said to his disciples about greatness. The child will memorize a Bible verse about humility. The lesson wraps up with the creation of a coat of arms that includes the verse, or another verse chosen from a given list, as his new motto.

Materials: New Testament
Lined paper and pen for copy work
List of Bible Verses for the Choleric Child
Drawing Paper
Colored pencils or markers

Preparation: For this particular story, it's important to use a Bible that has the verses noted in number 1 below. Many children's Bibles paraphrase or skip this material about John the Baptist, diminishing the significance of his story for choleric children. Review the sections in your favorite Bible before beginning the lesson to make sure it meets these requirements.

1. Read the story of John the Baptist.
Read John 1:19-42 and 3:22-40. Read it aloud to a child aged eight to ten. An older child can read it by himself or aloud to you as you choose.

2. Narrate.
A child aged eight to ten can give you an oral narration of the text, which you transcribe for him, word for word. If you are working with more than one child at a time, have the younger child tell you everything he can remember about the text first. Then the older child can add whatever details his sibling missed. You may choose to have an older child write his narration, or, if he has read the text

on his own, tell you orally what he considers the most important parts.

If you are unfamiliar with narrations, you can read more about them here: *charlottemasonhomeschooling.wordpress.com/charlotte-mason-methods/using-narration-in-your-charlotte-mason-homeschool/*

3. Define humility.
Tell your child that John the Baptist is a model of the virtue of humility. Ask him to define humility.

Here is Fr. John Hardon's definition (for your reference only):

> The moral virtue that keeps a person from reaching beyond himself. It is the virtue that restrains the unruly desire for personal greatness and leads people to an orderly love of themselves based on a true appreciation of their position with respect to God and their neighbors. Religious humility recognizes one's total dependence on God; moral humility recognizes one's creaturely equality with others. Yet humility is not only opposed to pride; it is also opposed to immoderate self-abjection, which would fail to recognize God's gifts and use them according to his will.[66]

Here is my simplified version of this definition for children:

> Humility is the virtue by which we recognize that we depend on God for everything—life, talents, possessions, health, and family. Humility reminds us that all people are made in God's image and have equal worth. It helps us not to think of ourselves as more important or greater than others, even when we have many good qualities. Humility is the opposite of pride. It also keeps us from thinking we are unworthy to be loved or that we are second rate. Humble people see the truth about themselves. They glorify God for everything they are and have.

---

[66] Fr. John Hardon, *Catholic Dictionary: an Abridged and Updated Version of Modern Catholic Dictionary,* (New York: Crown Publishing Group, 2013), 183.

4. Discuss

How did John the Baptist show that he was humble? What did he say? What did he do? *He said he was unworthy to baptize Jesus or to untie his sandals. He did not continue to protest after Jesus assured him it was right to baptize him. He wore simple clothes and ate simple food. He made it clear that he was not the Messiah, but just a servant. He said, "He must increase, but I must decrease," and he was content with that. He encouraged his disciples to leave him to follow Jesus. Etc.*

5. Copy and memory work

Copy and memorize this verse: "He must increase, but I must decrease." (Jn 3:30)

6. Create a coat of arms

A coat of arms is a design that was originally used to on armor that protected and identified medieval knights. In many cases, the coat of arms was passed down to a knight's children. Coats of arms were then modified slightly by different members of the family.

A complete coat of arms contains a shield (called an escutcheon), a helmet (or helm/coronet), supporters on each side of the shield, and a motto below the design.

Coat of arms template from Wikimedia Commons.

Tell your child: As you create a coat of arms, choose symbols that represent who you are and who you want to be.

Some symbols that have traditionally been associated with the choleric temperament are lions, bears, triangles, fire, summer, the color red, and the planet Mars.

Choose a verse about humility from the list of Bible Verses for the Choleric Child to make your motto. Then choose the supporters for your shield, colors, and symbols.

Lesson Plan 2: Becoming a Servant Leader

Ages: 8-14

Objective: The child will learn to lead by serving others.

Length of time: This lesson works well spread out over several days or weeks. You may want to do steps 1 and 2 the first day, then 3 and 4 on the next two days, and work on 5 for many weeks, doing 6 on the day you begin to practice servant leadership. Steps 7 and 8 should be used as you see fit over the next few years after the lesson has been completed.

Summary: The child will read *The Three Billy Goats Gruff* and two stories from the Gospels to help him understand the importance of leaders also being servants. (For girls or older children, if you prefer, you could read *Mother Teresa* by Demi. Adapt the lesson accordingly.) The lesson culminates with practice in servant leadership in the home. A written or oral paragraph at the beginning and end of the lesson helps the child express what true leadership entails. You can extend and strengthen the learning by helping the older child choose an ongoing service project outside the home, and guiding him towards reading about great men and women who have been servant leaders.

Materials: New Testament or children's Bible
Lined paper and pen for copy work
The Three Billy Goats Gruff by P. C. Asbjornsen, illustrated by Marcia Brown (or use the version in *The Moral Compass)* or
Mother Teresa by Demi

1. Introducing the topic
Have your child write a paragraph describing what kind of a leader he would like to be as he grows older. Younger children can narrate instead of writing.
Discuss: What leadership qualities do you have as a choleric?

2. The billy goats

Read *The Three Billy Goats Gruff* together or have an older child read it on his own.

Discuss:

1. How did the oldest billy goat look after his younger brothers?
2. Do you think he was a good leader?
3. What adjectives would you use to describe him?

3. The servant of all

Read Matthew 18:1-4 and 20:20-28 (Who is the greatest?)

Discuss:

1. Who represents the greatest in God's kingdom? *A child.*
2. How can we be like a child? *Being humble, trusting God, being dependent on God, etc.*
3. How else does Jesus talk about the greatest? *As a servant.*
4. How can a servant lead others? *By making sure everyone's needs are met, looking after the weak, helping others, etc.*
5. How do you think the oldest billy goat measured up to Jesus' standard of greatness?

Copy and memorize Matthew 20:26: "Whoever would be great among you must be your servant."

4. The washing of the feet

Read John 13:1-17

Discuss:

1. How did Jesus act like a servant? *He washed his disciples' feet.*
2. What was his biggest act of service? *Dying on the Cross.*
3. What's the greatest way we could serve others? *By dying for them.*
4. How can we "die" for our family members on a normal day? *We can make sacrifices for their good, put them before ourselves, etc.*

Give some examples of simple sacrifices your child can make, appropriate for his age, such as

- Sharing toys and books
- Spending time doing what the other person wants
- Praying and fasting

- Doing a siblings' chores
- Helping a toddler
- Encouraging and praising others

Now brainstorm together a list of specific sacrifices your child can make and things he can do for other family members.

5. Put it into practice
Choose one of the activities you brainstormed and have your child practice it daily until it becomes a habit. For example, "I will pour drinks for my little sister when she needs them without being asked." Older children (10+) may practice several types of servant leadership at once.

Cholerics love a challenge and love contests, even against themselves. Tap into this to motivate your child by having him keep track of how many times a day he practices being a servant leader. Offer a special reward when he reaches an agreed-upon goal. This works especially well for children who would like to be given more leadership responsibilities. "Because you have been faithful in a very little, you shall have authority over ten cities" (Luke 17:17).
Discuss:
1. How do you think your siblings will feel when you make sacrifices for them? *Good, happy, they will like me, etc.*
2. Would you rather follow a person who orders you around or one who helps you when you need help?

6. Write and discuss
Write a paragraph describing the ideal leader you would want to follow. Younger children can narrate instead of writing.
Discuss:
1. How is your ideal leader different from the leader that you said you would like to be at the start of this lesson?
2. Which one is more like a servant leader?
3. Which one is more like Jesus?
4. Which one do you think more people would want to follow?
5. Have your ideas about the kind of leader that you would like to be changed? If so, how?

7. Ongoing learning

Here are saints and modern heroes who are good models of servant leadership. To keep the lessons learned from being forgotten, assign your child to read about or research one of them now and then:

- St. Louis
- Helen Keller
- St. Maximilian Kolbe
- Mary Jo Copeland
- Pope Francis

Here are some questions to write about or discuss:

1. How is/was this person a servant leader?
2. What is/was his or her profession or vocation?
3. Give examples of service in that role.
4. How is/was he or she different from what you would normally expect of someone in that profession or vocation?
5. How can you be more like him or her?
6. How are you already alike?
7. What did you most like about this person?
8. Was there anything you didn't like?
9. Does/Did he or she have a choleric temperament? How can you tell?

Notes: When my choleric son (12) practiced servant leadership, his relationship with his youngest brother (then 3) completely turned around. As he made a habit of serving his brother in order to gain points, he became the preschooler's favorite sibling. Before this they had struggled to get along.

If you are concerned about offering a reward as a motivator, see my discussion of this in chapter 5.

Lesson Plan 3: Thinking before Speaking

Ages: 6-8

Objective: The child will practice stopping himself before cutting others down.

Length of time: Spread this lesson over the course of one school week.

Summary: The child will read Charles Perrault's fairy tale *Diamonds and Toads*. Then he will wear a diamond or toad card around his neck for a limited time after he says something particularly nice or uses his words badly. The choleric will enjoy this most if some of his siblings participate with him.

Materials: A well-illustrated version of *Diamonds and Toads* or the version in *The Book of Virtues*
The diamond and toad clip art at the end of chapter 13
Scissors
Single-hole punch
String

1. Introducing the topic
Ask your child to remember the last time someone insulted him or cut him down. What did that person say? How did it make your child feel? How often does he speak too quickly, saying something he shouldn't, because he hasn't thought it through?

2. Read aloud together.
Read *Diamonds and Toads* together.
Discuss:
    1.   How is this fairy tale similar to others the child is more familiar with? *Like* Cinderella, *there is an evil stepmother and stepsister. Virtue is rewarded. Like* Beauty and the Beast *an enchantress poses as a poor old woman to test characters' virtue. Etc.*

2. How is it different? *There is only one stepsister, there is no prince, etc.*
3. Why did the first daughter have jewels fall from her mouth and the second have toads and snakes? *The first was kind and the second was selfish and greedy.*
4. What would it be like for you to have diamonds or toads come out of your mouth every time you spoke? *You could be rich or be an outcast, rewarding or embarrassing, etc.*
5. Our words can be like diamonds or toads to other people. What types of words are like diamonds? *Kindness, compliments, encouragement, etc.*
6. What types of words are like toads or snakes? *Insults, bad language, complaining, gossiping, backtalk, etc.*

3. Make diamond and toad necklaces.
Print as many copies of the diamond and toad clipart as you need. Have your child cut them into rectangular cards, then hole-punch the top two corners. Finally, he can thread a piece of string about eighteen inches long through the holes and tie the ends together, so he can wear the appropriate card around his neck.

4. Practice thinking before speaking.
For the next few days, reward every kind thing your child says by letting him wear the diamond around his neck for an hour afterward. If he insults someone else, talks back, uses bad language, gossips, or complains, he must wear a toad card for one hour.

5. Wrap up discussion.
Ask your child: How did you feel when you wore the diamond? How did you feel when you wore the toad? How did the rest of the family like it when you tried so hard to say something nice all the time? Try to remember to keep practicing this, even without the diamond and toad cards.

6. Extra fun.
You can find coloring pages for this story online at *www.kids-pages.com*

There is even a student opera available for the story, if you have lots of girls in your home or your homeschool group. See *www.greaterworcesteropera.org/*

Lesson Plan 4: Learning Empathy

Ages: 10-14

Objective: The child will form the habit of recognizing and interpreting others' emotional cues.

Summary: Beginning with watching the expressions and gestures of actors in a movie, your child will correlate these with emotions, then move to drawing faces with different emotions and writing a story with characters using these expressions. Finally, he will practice asking others about their feelings in non-tense moments.

Materials: DVD of one of the following: *The Secret Garden, Where the Red Fern Grows, Mr. Smith Goes to Washington, Cranford,* or another live-action movie that conveys a whole range of emotions and is appropriate for your child's age and sex.

Instructions on drawing facial expressions, such as this one: *danidraws.com/blog/2007/12/06/50-facial-expressions-and-how-to-draw-them/*

Drawing paper

Drawing pencil and eraser

Pen and paper

Word processing program for writing a story (optional)

A book that demonstrates the principle of showing, not telling, emotion. Suggestions: *How Many Days to America?* by Eve Bunting, *Fireflies* by Julie Brinckloe, *Baseball Saved Us* by Ken Mochizuki, or *Butterfly* by Patricia Polacco. These books are written for younger grades, but illustrate the principle of showing, not telling, beautifully. Feel free to choose longer works for an older child.

Preparation: No real preparation necessary.

1. Note the emotional cues in a movie.

Watch your chosen movie scene by scene, or in a group of scenes no more than ten minutes long. Observe the facial expressions and gestures of the actors. Pause the movie, then discuss how these gestures are used to portray specific emotions. Write them down, followed by the character's name. For example:

Wrinkled forehead - anger (Mary Lennox)

Continue on in this way until the end of the movie (or as much of it as you think necessary for this exercise) has been analyzed.

2. Discuss the patterns.

Was each character consistent with his emotional cues? How did the characters differ from one another? Does anyone in your family use these expressions or gestures?

3. Draw the expressions.

Draw several of the facial expressions, using the instruction suggested above or a drawing book. For extra fun, all the children in your family can draw twenty-four expressions of their choosing from the examples, in the form of a BINGO card. Leave the middle space of the card as a free space.

3. Read a story.

Read a book such as those suggested in the materials section, in which the author portrays emotions with expressions, descriptive words, and gestures, rather than by naming them. Discuss the emotions portrayed and the words used to do so.

4. Write a short story.

Write your own story that is the length of one chapter in a book (3-10 pages, depending on the child's age and writing experience). Show, don't tell, the characters' emotions.

5. Discuss your child's desires.

How do you want others to respond when you are angry? Sad? Disappointed? Frustrated? Anxious? Excited? Jealous? (As the parent, model these reactions if possible.)

6. Ask others about their emotions.
For the next two weeks, watch for emotional cues in those around you. If you see someone wrinkle his forehead, ask if he is frustrated. Can you do anything to help? If someone's face turns red, ask if he is angry. Can you compromise with him? If someone walks away, ask if he needs a break. (The parent should emphasize doing this with tact. You may want to discuss this project with other family members and try to get everyone on board with it, suggesting that your choleric is trying to learn so he can be more sensitive in the future. Don't let this turn into a way for him to control others.)

7. Extra fun.
Watch a classic silent film such as *Peter Pan, Our Gang,* or *The Thief of Bagdad* (online free at *archive.org/details/ThiefOfBagdad1924*). Each child in the family can use his BINGO card to record the emotions portrayed. See who gets BINGO first.

Lesson Plan 5: Corporal Works of Mercy

Ages: 10–16

Objective: The child will choose a corporal work of mercy to pursue.

Summary: After memorizing the corporal works of mercy, the child will learn how a saint, his parents, and others in his community have practiced these works. Then he will begin practicing them at home and in his community.

Materials: New Testament
Lined paper and pen for copy work
Memorize the Faith by Kevin Vost (optional)
Book about St. Martin de Porres, or *Mother Teresa* by Demi.

Preparation: Buy or borrow a book about St. Martin de Porres or Blessed Mother Teresa of Calcutta, as appropriate for your child's age and sex. Research opportunities to practice the corporal works of mercy in your town or community.

1. Read Matthew 25:31-46
Read the passage aloud to a younger child. Your child ages 12 and up can read it on his own.

2. List the corporal works of mercy.
Together or separately, have the child find and list the corporal works of mercy as found in the passage. Afterward, read this passage from *Youcat (Youth Catechism of the Catholic Church):*

> What are the "corporal works of mercy"?
>
> To feed the hungry, give drink to the thirsty, clothe the naked, shelter the homeless, visit the sick and the imprisoned, and bury the dead. (450)

Ask: How does your list compare to the list in the Catechism?

3. Memory and copy work

Memorize the corporal works of mercy in order. Use the method found in *Memorize the Faith* if you wish. Write them in your neatest handwriting and display them in your home.

4. For the parent: Modeling the works of mercy.

As the parent, share with your child ways you have practiced and are practicing the corporal works of mercy. Do you give regularly to an organization that helps the poor? Did you go on a mission trip as a teenager? Do you or your spouse participate in charitable activities through your employer? Tell any stories you have that your child may find exciting or inspiring. Do you have photos of a special project that you can look at together? Why did you choose to serve in this particular way?

5. Read about a charitable saint.

Together or separately, read about the life of St. Martin de Porres or Blessed Teresa of Calcutta. Write or tell orally the story of one person whom the saint helped. The child ages 8 to 12 can draw a picture illustrating the book as well.

6. Practice the works of mercy at home.

Brainstorm ways you can practice the corporal works of mercy in your home. Examples: give the toddler his breakfast, make dinner one night so Mom can get a break, go through your clothes and choose some to give to the poor, do the chores of a sibling who doesn't feel good.

7. Practice the works of mercy in your community.

Is there a food shelf, soup kitchen, or other facility to help the poor in your area that you can visit as a family? Investigate opportunities to practice the corporal works of mercy in your town. Choose together one activity you can do regularly to serve the less fortunate. Make a firm commitment, putting it on your calendar.

CHAPTER 14

Templates

For an 8½ by 11 version of the Spiritual Growth Plan Templates, subscribe to my email list at ContemplativeHomeschool.com.

Teaching Your Choleric Child Humility

"The most powerful weapon to conquer the Devil is humility. For, as he does not know at all how to employ it, neither does he know how to defend himself from it."

–St. Vincent de Paul

Name_____ Date _____

Assess: Describe your child's pride.

_____
_____
_____
_____
_____
_____
_____
_____
_____
_____
_____
_____

Create goals: How would you like your child to grow in humility by the end of this year?

_____
_____
_____
_____
_____
_____
_____
_____
_____
_____
_____
_____

Choose methods and materials: How will you help your child towards these goals?

_____
_____
_____
_____
_____
_____
_____
_____
_____
_____
_____
_____
_____
_____
_____

Review: What progress did your child make in humility? Where does he still need to grow?

_____
_____
_____
_____
_____
_____
_____
_____
_____
_____
_____
_____
_____
_____

Teaching Your Choleric Child Compassion

"Compassion begins at home, and it is not how much we do but how much love we put in that action."

-Blessed Teresa of Calcutta

Name_____ Date _____

Assess: Describe your child's compassion

_____
_____
_____
_____
_____
_____
_____
_____
_____
_____
_____

Create goals: How would you like your child to grow in compassion by the end of this year?

_____
_____
_____
_____
_____
_____
_____
_____
_____
_____
_____
_____
_____

Choose methods and materials: How will you help your child towards these goals?

_____
_____
_____
_____
_____
_____
_____
_____
_____
_____
_____
_____
_____
_____
_____
_____
_____

Review: What progress did your child make in compassion? Where does he still need to grow?

_____
_____
_____
_____
_____
_____
_____
_____
_____
_____
_____
_____
_____
_____
_____
_____

Teaching Your Choleric Child to Think before Acting

"Take pains to refrain from sharp words. If they escape your lips, do not be ashamed to let your lips produce the remedy, since they have caused the wounds."

–St. Francis of Paola

Name_____ Date _____

Assess: Describe your child's tendency to act without thinking.

_____
_____
_____
_____
_____
_____
_____
_____
_____
_____

Create goals: How would you like your child to grow in thinking before acting by the end of this year?

_____
_____
_____
_____
_____
_____
_____
_____
_____
_____
_____
_____

Choose methods and materials: How will you help your child towards these goals?

_____

_____

_____

_____

_____

_____

_____

_____

_____

_____

_____

_____

_____

_____

_____

_____

Review: What progress did your child make in thinking before acting? Where does he still need to grow?

_____

_____

_____

_____

_____

_____

_____

_____

_____

_____

_____

_____

_____

_____

Teaching Your Choleric Child Respect and Obedience

"Blessed indeed are the obedient, for God will never permit them to go astray."

-St. Francis De Sales

Name_____ Date _____

Assess: Describe your child's level of respect and obedience.

_____
_____
_____
_____
_____
_____
_____
_____
_____
_____

Create goals: How would you like your child to grow in respect and obedience by the end of this year?

_____
_____
_____
_____
_____
_____
_____
_____
_____
_____
_____
_____
_____
_____
_____

Choose methods and materials: How will you help your child towards these goals?

Choose methods and materials: How will you help your child towards these goals?

Review: What progress did your child make in respect and obedience? Where does he still need to grow?

Clip art for Lesson Plan 3

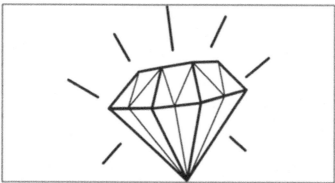

Toad courtesy of Free Clip Art Now, Diamond courtesy ClipArtBest.com

Afterward

I trust that by now you have a better understanding of your choleric child, his motivation, strengths, and weaknesses. As I said at the beginning, he is destined to have a lasting impact on the world. Whether that impact is for good or for evil depends on the choices he makes. Will he use his gifts for God's glory? Will he learn to humbly listen to others? Will he be a leader who serves, rather than one who lords over those under him?

You cannot make his choices for him. More than those of any other temperament, the choleric will go his own way. But with the graces of holy matrimony, you and your spouse can help him to embrace God's way as his own. You can be his models in prayer and virtue, teaching him to make a growing relationship with God his top priority in life. Once he has set this as his goal, virtually no one will be able to turn him aside from it.

As your sister in Christ and a fellow parent striving to lead my children toward holiness, I will be praying for you and your child. When you are frustrated with his foibles, remember that God desires his spiritual growth even more than you do. He made your child to be a saint. Be patient. Be prayerful. Be loving. Be ready to share an eternity in heaven with this awesome gift God has given you—your choleric child!

Bibliography

Aumann, Jordan, OP. *Spiritual Theology. archive.org/stream-/SpiritualTheologyByFr.JordanAumannO.p/AumannO.p.SpiritualTheologyall_djvu.txt* (accessed April 12, 2015).

Baron, Renee. *What Type am I? Discover Who You Really Are.* New York: Penguin, 1998.

Bennett, Art, and Laraine Bennett. *The Temperament God Gave You: The Classic Key to Knowing Yourself, Getting along with Others, and Growing Closer to the Lord.* Manchester, NH: Sophia Institute Press, 2005.

Carey, William B., M.D., and Martha Jablow. *Understanding Your Child's Temperament.* New York: MacMillan, 1997.

Carter, Dr. Les. *The Anger Trap.* San Francisco: Jossey-Bass, 2003.

Catechism of the Catholic Church (2nd ed.). Washington, DC.: Libreria Editrice Vaticana-United States Conference of Catholic Bishops, 2000.

Groeschel, Benedict J. *Spiritual Passages: the Psychology of Spiritual Development.* New York: The Crossroad Publishing Co., 2004.

Guarendi, Dr. Ray, and David Eich. *Back to the Family: Proven Advice on Building a Stronger, Healthier, Happier Family.* New York: Simon and Schuster, 1991.

Hardon, Fr. John. *Catholic Dictionary: an Abridged and Updated Version of Modern Catholic Dictionary.* New York: Crown Publishing Group, 2013.

Hey Parents—Teach Them About Real Love! Parent Handbook on Human Sexuality. Diocese of La Crosse, Wisconsin, 2003.

Hock, Fr. Conrad. *The Four Temperaments and the Spiritual Life.* Milwaukee: The Pallotine Fathers, 1934.

www.catholicapologetics.info/catholicteaching/virtue/temperaments. htm (accessed April 12, 2015).

John Paul II. *Familiaris consortio,* Apostolic Exhortation on the Role of the Christian Family in the Modern World. Vatican Web site. November 22, 1981. *w2.vatican.va/content/john-paul-ii/en/apost_exhortations/documents/hf_jp-ii_exh_19811122_familiaris-consortio.html* (accessed April 12, 2015).

Keogh, Barbara K. *Temperament in the Classroom.* Baltimore: Brookes Publishing, 2003.

Kurcinka, Mary Sheedy. *Kids, Parents, and Power Struggles.* New York: HarperCollins, 2001.

Kurcinka, Mary Sheedy. *Raising Your Spirited Child.* New York: HarperCollins, 1998.

LaHaye, Tim. *Spirit-Controlled Temperament.* La Mesa, CA: Post, 1992.

Littauer, Florence. *Personality Plus for Couples: Understanding Yourself and the One You Love.* Grand Rapids, MI: F.H. Revell, 2001.

Rowan, Chris, OTR, "The Impact of Technology on Child Sensory and Motor Development." *www.sensomotorische-integratie.nl/CrisRowan.pdf* (accessed April 12, 2015).

Schonnburn, Cardinal Christoph, editor. *Youcat: Youth Catechism of the Catholic Church.* San Francisco: Ignatius Press, 2011.

Warfield, Hal. "Temperament and Personality," *Self-Growth.* *www.selfgrowth.com/articles/Warfield2.html* (accessed April 12, 2015).

Vasicek, Ed. "Temperament Theory," *Highland Park Church.* *www.highlandpc.com/articles/temptheo.php* (accessed April 8, 2015).

Acknowledgments

I thank God for all who have helped me with their work, prayers, and advice in writing and publishing this book, especially my husband, Dan Rossini; my children, who were the guinea pigs for the ideas and lesson plans; the members of my non-fiction critique group; my beta readers, Jeannie Ewing and Missy Fillion; Patti Maguire Armstrong; the members of my Google Plus Community, Indie Catholic Authors; and all who participated in my book blog tour or wrote a review. This book is a tribute to your support and hard work on my behalf.

About the Author

Connie Rossini lives with her husband Dan in New Ulm, Minnesota, where she homeschools their four sons. Her spirituality column, God Alone Suffices, is published in *The Prairie Catholic* of the Diocese of New Ulm. She is the author of *Trusting God with St. Therese* and the free ebook *Five Lessons from the Carmelite Saints That Will Change Your Life*. She blogs on Carmelite spirituality and raising prayerful kids at ContemplativeHomeschool.com and is a columnist at SpiritualDirection.com. She also owns the Google Plus Community Indie Catholic Authors.

Join Connie's readers' list at ContemplativeHomeschool.com for free materials to help your whole family grow in holiness.

Made in the USA
Las Vegas, NV
13 June 2022